COMIC, CURIOUS & QUIRKY

NEWS STORIES
FROM CENTURIES PAST

COMIC, CURIOUS & QUIRKY

NEWS STORIES
FROM CENTURIES PAST

Rona Levin

The British Library

ACKNOWLEDGEMENTS

With special thanks to David Way, Publisher at the British Library, for all his help and support, without whom this book would not have been possible. Thanks also to Brightsolid and the British Library for their wonderful newspaper archive.

First published in 2014 by
The British Library
96 Euston Road
London NW1 2DB

This paperback edition published in 2016

© 2014, 2016 Rona Levin

British Library Cataloguing in Publication Data
A CIP Record for this book is available
from The British Library

ISBN 978 0 7123 5659 6

Designed by
Briony Hartley, Goldust Design
Printed and bound by
CPI Group (UK) Ltd, Croydon CR0 4YY

For my father Arthur, late mother Eve,
Nia, Mark, Michael, Samantha and Penny.
Thank you for putting up with me.

CONTENTS

INTRODUCTION

Whilst researching in the British Library's digitised Newspaper Archive I have found it utterly engrossing to be able to step back in time and gain insight into the social mores, preoccupations and sensibilities of society over the 200 years covered here. The eclectic items that made the final selection all struck me in some way as being quirkily strange or amusing, although sometimes, admittedly, for all the wrong reasons. In that vein, as well as entertaining the reader, I hope that the content may also prove to be somewhat thought-provoking, serving to reflect the trials, tribulations and perils of day-to-day life in those times.

As an aside, the more pedantic amongst you will observe that, despite the book's subtitle being *News Stories from Centuries Past*, I have in fact slipped in (just a few) advertisements and Letters to the Editor that particularly caught my eye, simply because, like news stories, they serve to illustrate the issues and values of the day, so I trust I shall be forgiven for slightly veering away from my remit.

Hopefully, these stories will resonate with readers for many different reasons. Some illustrate just how little the times may be seen to have changed in terms of working life, crime and gossip – from horsemeat fraud to a policeman breaking his leg after treading on orange peel. Other stories highlight the opposite, showing what life was like before the days of health and safety and other regulatory constraints, for better or worse – usually for the much, much worse, as many stories will doubtless demonstrate.

The surprisingly gory details frequently given in descriptions of people's tragic demise is also noteworthy, being far more explicit than today's newspapers would allow, with sentences such as "a quantity of blood and brains dropped from the wound" or "his body was found stretched on the bed, and his brains lying in different parts of the room".

Nor were newspapers from centuries ago as deferential to royalty as we might suppose. The report of the death of the Empress Maria Theresa of Vienna is a prime example, stating that when her body was cut open there was found to be "much fat and viscous matter which is attributed to Her Majesty having accustomed herself, from her youth, never to spit". It would be unthinkable to imagine newspapers of modern times reporting similar detail at the time of our own beloved late Queen Mother's death.

Sexual diseases and their consequences were also written about in newspapers quite plainly, long before the supposedly prudish Victorian era, with explicit descriptions of symptoms and cures. Even during Victorian times, the custom of wearing false "bozoms" to lure men was commented upon in the press (as was the ladies fashion of wearing false latex ears to cover "coarse" ears).

My time researching this book certainly made me reflect not only on the human drama behind the news stories, but also on the laborious processes involved in establishing the newsgathering, production and distribution networks for the newspapers, long before today's modern means of communication.

Spare a thought especially for the logistics that must have been involved in foreign newsgathering, acquiring eye-witness reports or reproducing stories published in newspapers abroad, which may then have taken many months to reach the UK from distant lands.

On a final note, I would encourage everyone to travel back to another time through the pages of the British Library's newspaper archives – it is a truly addictive experience.

www. britishnewspaperarchive.co.uk

RONA LEVIN,
June 2014

DASTARDLY DEEDS
AND DEADLY DESIRES

Derby Mercury, 29 July 1748

WAS THIS LORD CHIEF JUSTICE A COWBOY JUDGE?

One Balls was tried this Bedford Assizes, before the Lord Chief Justice Willes, for tying a boy to a cow, which running away, dragged him along, and breaking his back and most of his bones, killed him before anybody came to his assistance: but it appearing not to be maliciously done, he was acquitted.

Police Gazette, 17 February 1775

BRAINLESS DEED OF DESPAIR IN GORY DETAIL

On the 15th inst. a dragoon belonging to Gen. Carpenter's regiment, having been drinking at the Green Man between Leiston and Aldeburgh with some farmers of that neighbourhood, all of a sudden he was missed out of the room, but upon the report of a pistol, and some blood running through the ceiling into the kitchen, an alarm was given, and assistance called; when, upon going up into his chamber his body was found stretched on the bed, and his brains lying in different parts of the room. The cause of this rash action is supposed to his having shot a smuggler about year ago, when on a party against them.

Hereford Journal, 4 January 1781

SPITTING IMAGE – EMPRESS'S EXPIRATION DUE TO LACK OF EXPECTORATION

Vienna, December 9. The body of the late Empress [Maria Theresa, last of the House of Hapsburg and mother of Queen Marie Antoinette of France] was opened on the 30th of last month, and it afforded matter of astonishment that she did not die of a dropsy [swelling of soft tissues due to the accumulation of excess water], as was believed, no water being found in the breast, but a great quantity of fat and viscous matter, which is attributed to Her Majesty having accustomed herself, from her youth, never to spit. The resignation of that great Princess has been much admired; for, the nature of her disorder not permitting her to lie on a bed, she was obliged to rest on a sofa, almost always in the same position, which was extremely uneasy.

Aberdeen Journal, 2 January 1798

A CALL TO ARMS AND SLAVE TO FOLLY
BY CAPTAIN BLUNDERBUSS

Bridgetown, Barbados, October 14, 1797. On Tuesday afternoon last, drifted on shore on the north east part of this island, a boat with two men and a boy. Of all human sufferings, few, if any, can exceed what these miserable, ill-fated mortals experienced, nor can dangers equal what they encountered, at the recital of which our blood freezes, and our feelings cannot but be deeply distressed at the relation of such a sense of human misery.

These are part of a crew belonging to the ship *Thomas*, [under Captain] M'Quay, of Liverpool, on his middle voyage from the coast of Africa to this land. From that coast being infected with French privateers, Capt. M'Quay had taught his male slaves the use of arms, in order that they should aid him to repel the attacks of the enemy, should any be made, as he had frequent skirmishes on his last voyage.

But instead of becoming auxiliaries in his defence, they took advantage of his instructions, and seizing his ammunition chest, on the 2nd of September, early in the morning, about 200 of them appeared on deck, accoutred, and fired on the crew, some of whom fell, others in dismay leaped overboard, who were also fired at, whilst others cut away the boat lashed to her stern, and took refuge in her by escaping through the cabin windows, leaving the Captain and the rest of the crew endeavouring to quell the insurgents, by discharging such arms as are usually kept in cabins.

But upon the Captain's observing that some were in the boats and about to desert the ship, he remonstrated so warmly as to induce them to return, but they, perceiving that they were overpowered, and seeing no possibility of escaping the danger that awaited them, again severed the boat, and quitted the ship; of these there were 12.

Having fled from the fury of savage ferocity they now became a prey to the winds and waves, to hunger and thirst, and after having suffered the horrors of these for some days, they providentially took a small turtle, while floating asleep on the surface of the water, which they devoured, and again being driven to distress for want of food, they soaked their shoes, and two hairy caps, which were among them, in the water, which being rendered soft, each partook of them.

But day after day having past, and the cravings of hunger passing hard upon them, they fell upon the dreadful, horrible expedient of eating each other: and to prevent any contention about who should become the food for others, they cast lots, when he on whom the lot fell, with manly fortitude resigned to his life, with the persuasion of his body becoming the means of existence to his companions in distress, but solicited that he might be bled to death, (the surgeon being with them and having his instruments in his pocket when he left the ship).

No sooner had the fatal instrument touched the vein, then the operator applied his parched lips and drank of the blood that flowed, whilst the rest anxiously watched his departing breath, that they might satisfy the hunger than gnawed them. Those that gutted themselves with human flesh, and human gore, and whose stomachs retained the unnatural food, soon perished from raging insanity, from putrification, as we conceive, superseding the digestion.

Thus, the dreary prospect became the more so to the survivors, from seeing their fellow companions expire before them, from the very cause that ravenous hunger impelled them to imagine would give them existence.

Those that remained attribute the preservation of their lives to having rejected following the example of their fellow sufferers. Indeed they assert having refused risking their lives to the chance of a straw, but the majority having determined it, they could not refuse. Our narrator, a Mr Farmer, has not furnished us with the time when the death of the others took place.

Cambridge Chronicle and Journal, 1 January 1813

FARMER'S EXPLOITS BRING THE HOUSE DOWN

On Saturday se'nnight [the previous Saturday], Mr. Woodier, a farmer from the parish of Lovaton [Devon], having purchased 20lbs [9 kgs] weight of gunpowder in Ashburton, took it in a bag to the shop of Mr. Chalk, blacksmith, and while waiting for his horse untied the mouth of the bag to put in a stone for the purpose of balancing the weight; unfortunately a spark of fire from the anvil communicated to the powder, which instantly blew up the house and another adjoining. Chalk, his apprentice, and three children, were buried in the ruins but were dug out without sustaining material injury. Woodier had an arm broken. The crash was tremendous, and the shock was felt throughout the town.

Taunton Courier, and Western Advertiser, 24 May 1820

ACTOR GUNNING FOR FAME FINDS IT!

A serious accident occurred at the Carnarvon Theatre a few evenings since, during the performance of the melodrama called *The Miller and his Men*. In the scene where Grindolf, the miller, throws off his disguise, the actor who performed that part unfortunately got his pistols entangled in the folds of his cloak, in consequence of which one of them went off, and the wadding penetrating his belly, he fell as if dead. Surgeons were called in, and the wound was dressed, and distant hopes are entertained of his recovery.

Bath Chronicle and Weekly Gazette, 14 January 1830

SAVED BY A WHISKER… MAN'S FATE NEARLY SEALED!

Last week, as a young man, undeterred by the inclemency of the weather, was bathing off the pier of Leith [Scotland], he was mistaken for a seal, and shot at. He escaped, however, without injury.

Northampton Mercury, 11 September 1830

FATAL RECIPE FOR A DINNER-DATE
WHICH DIDN'T PAN OUT

On Thursday last, Mrs Shaw, wife of Thomas Shaw, mercer and draper, boiled a leg of mutton for the dinner of her family, in a saucepan which had some days previous been used to boil arsenic for the purpose of destroying vermin. When the dinner was prepared, Mrs Shaw sent part of the broth to a young man who was unwell, and partook of some herself.

The Rev. John Hughes, Wesleyan Minister, having called in, was invited to dinner. He and Mr Shaw sat down, and were in the act of eating the broth, when Mrs Shaw was taken suddenly ill; and, as the use previously made of the saucepan in which she prepared the broth returned to her mind, she desired them to eat no more.

A messenger was immediately dispatched for medical assistance. The unfortunate woman lingered in great pain until Saturday evening, when she expired. The young man, to whom part of it had been sent, discovered its poisonous quality and threw it from his stomach, as did also the Rev. John Hughes. They are out of danger, but Mr Shaw continues to be very ill.

Bucks Herald, 5 January 1833

WHAT SEEMED AT FIRST HARMLESS MADE BOY ARMLESS

Accident from Gunpowder. On Saturday last a son of Mr Thomas Stanton, baker, from Newport Pagnell, was amusing himself in the bake-house with a flask of powder by dropping a few grains on some embers, when the whole flask was ignited, and shockingly lacerated his hand and arm as to render amputation necessary.

Wiltshire Independent, 16 August 1838

IF ONLY THE TRAGIC VICTIM HAD SAT ON THE FENCE HEDGING HER BETS

A singular and fatal accident occurred at Cold Ashton, near Marshfield, on Wednesday, to a young girl, about 15 years of age, named Charlotte Williams. She was on a visit to her uncle, who keeps the White Hart, at Ashton, and had been in the hay-field adjoining the house, and was sitting on the gate of the field, bearing a hay-fork in her hand with the prongs pointing towards her body, when, by some jar or movement of the gate, she fell forwards, and one of the prongs of the fork entered near her right breast, and, passing upwards, divided the carotid artery, and the poor girl bled to death in a few minutes. Verdict: Accidental death.

Windsor and Eton Express, 2 March 1839

FOOTLOOSE AND FANCY FREE

A man, who had drunk freely of beer and spirits, swallowed an ounce of laudanum. He was taken to the Middlesex Hospital, where the stomach-pump was used, and recourse afterwards had to flagellation, the bastinado [instrument for foot-whipping], and cold douche, followed by the application of a cayenne plaster to the pit of the stomach. The man, though insensible for many hours, eventually recovered. To such an extent was it found necessary to use the bastinado that the soles of the feet mortified.

SERIOUSLY IMPRACTICAL JOKE

A foolish fellow, named Bishop, a bricklayer, employed at Clay Cross Railway Works, committed the following act of folly, called a practical joke: He took a shovel-full of lighted coals from the fire at the works, and threw them into a cart containing a barrel of gunpowder, which exploded, throwing the silly fellow to a distance of 20 yards [18.28 metres], tearing the clothes from off his back, and dreadfully wounding and scorching him.

Leamington Spa Courier, 4 May 1839

BALLOON TRIAL WORKERS RISE TO THE CHALLENGE

An accident, which very nearly attended with the loss of several persons' lives, occurred on Monday evening through the mismanagement of some parties concerned in a trial of a new balloon. It will be recollected, that last summer an attempt was made to inflate a large balloon in the Surrey Zoological Gardens, but not being successful it was entirely destroyed by the disappointed spectators.

It appears that the projector, Mr. Hoare, has since, at great expense, constructed another of still larger dimensions, but the proprietor of the Surrey Gardens being determined that no more attempts of the kind should be made in those grounds, a new site was fixed upon the Beulah Spa, Norwood; and on Monday night an experimental inflation took place, preparatory to an ascent at the opening of the Croydon Railway.

A large stage having been erected for the purpose in an adjoining meadow, the inflation was commenced, a number of men being employed in holding the vast machine. In the space of 12 minutes the balloon was completely filled with heated air, generated in a furnace, from chopped straw, birch, and alder wood; the ascending power suddenly became so great, that in removing the machine away from the furnace, it escaped from the hands of most of the men, ascended to great height, taking up five persons clinging to the ropes and sides of the car.

One of these, a youth whose name we did not learn, when about 30 feet [9.14 metres] from the ground, could hold on no longer, fell, and was much injured. The others remained clinging to the balloon, and were conveyed about one mile, when the machine, having lost its power by the condensation of the contained air, descended in the midst of a field.

The principal gardener belonging to Beulah Spa, Wm. Stevens, having let go his hold, got his foot entangled with rope, and was thus suspended with his head downwards for several minutes. When the balloon reached the earth his leg was found to be completely severed, being attached by the tendons only. It has since been amputated, but he lies in dangerous state.

One man was caught by the grapnel [tethering device with multiple hooks for grasping], and was seriously torn. The other two, although much cut and bruised, have received no material injuries.

Mr. Hoare himself is not hurt, and purposes making another attempt, but it is to be hoped that the patronage of the public, which has long encouraged these useless and dangerous exhibitions, will be turned into more safe and rational channels. The balloon remains in the field where it fell, and has not received much damage.

Belfast News-Letter, 22 August 1843

ROWING ROW LANDS CREW IN HOT WATER

A melancholy occurrence at The Coleraine Regatta [Northern Ireland]. We regret to state, that, shortly after the conclusion of the third race on Wednesday last, a misunderstanding took place between the crew of an Ennishowen boat and a Portrush boat, which came to blows. Oars were used, on both sides, as weapons, and one poor fellow, named Stewart, on board the Ennishowen boat received a blow on the head, which knocked him into the water, from where his body was not recovered for upwards of an hour. When the body was found, every means were adopted to restore animation, but in vain. The crew of the Portrush boat were immediately taken into custody, and we understand that since the melancholy transaction took place, the individual who inflicted the blows on Stewart has been committed for trial – the remainder of the crew were discharged.

Bath Chronicle and Weekly Gazette, 24 April 1851

A BLINDING SOLUTION EXECUTED WITH MILITARY PRECISION

Lately, a man confined in Haddington prison on a charge of poaching was found out to be a deserter from the army, and being apprehensive that he would be handed over to the military tribunal at the expiry of his sentence, he induced his fellow prisoner to puncture his eye with a needle to cause blindness, so that he may no longer be fit to serve His Majesty. This was so effectually done that he lost sight of his right eye entirely.

DID THIS PEELER'S SLIP-UP SEE HIM APPEAL FOR COMPENSATION?

One of the Gloucester police, when walking down Northgate Street, on Thursday evening last, in consequence of treading on a piece of orange peel, fell and broke his leg.

Wells Journal, 20 September 1851

A BAD WAY TO GET PLASTERED

The chief physician at the Royal Hospital in Vienna, Dr. Reyer, was conversing one day with his colleagues as to the least painful form of death, apparently in good health and spirits at the time; yet that evening he was found in his room a corpse, having put an end to his existence by fastening a bladder filled with chloroform round his mouth and nostrils by means of a band of plaster.

Hampshire Advertiser, 11 November 1854.

ALL SNUFFED OUT BY FIREWORKS AFTER SNUFFING OUT A CANDLE

On Monday morning a terrific explosion took place on the premises of Mr John Watson firework maker of Cannon Street, St George's-in-the-East, whereby three children perished and five individuals were so extensively burned and otherwise injured that great fears are entertained of their ultimate recovery.

The deceased when discovered were in a frightful condition, the arms and legs being entirely destroyed. The heads were crushed in, and the bodies literally burned to a blackened and charred mass. It seems that one of the older daughters had been engaged in filling in and finishing off the fireworks when she snuffed out a candle burning on the table, and a spark falling on some composition she was using, the same took fire and rapidly communicated to various piles of other pyrotechnics.

BARELY BELIEVABLE – NAKED MAN DIVES INTO FURNACE

At Leeds, on Monday last, a young man named George Towler, a miner, who had for some time past laboured under an aberration of intellect, flung himself, in a state of nudity, head foremost into a glowing furnace, which was at that moment filled with 50 tons

[50,802 kgs] of molten iron. Every effort was made to drag the body out, but all that remained of the unhappy suicide, consisted only of the vertebrae and skull, so blackened and contorted by the action of the fire as to render its recognition as part of anything human quite impossible.

Royal Cornwall Gazette, 17 November 1854

ONE-WAY TICKET TO HEAVEN BUT TRAVELLING THIRD-CLASS ALL THE WAY

[The London Necropolis Railway, opened in 1854, was built to transport cadavers and mourners from a Waterloo terminus to its own cemetery in Woking, Surrey, at the time the largest in the world, built to ease the over-congestion of the city's burial grounds.

The plans were not without resistance. According to *The Fortean Times*, the Bishop of London, said: "It may sometimes happen that persons of opposite characters might be carried in the same conveyance. For instance, the body of some profligate spendthrift might be placed in a conveyance with the body of some respectable member of the church, which would shock the feelings of his friends." Burials and transportation of bodies and mourners were subsequently offered in first, second or third-class.]

A few years ago, the idea of founding a cemetery for the metropolis which should be more than 20 miles distant from it, would have been looked upon as an absurdity; but this important experiment has now been formally carried out. Among the various uses of railways, it was an ingenious and happy idea to include that of making them to conduce at once to the comfort and health of the living and the orderly and decent performance of the last obsequies for the dead, by removing public cemeteries to a sufficient distance from the precincts of crowded cities.

The land purchased by the company exceeds 2,100 acres [850 hectares] in extent... The size of this tract will be best understood when it is stated that the total area of the existing suburban cemeteries are only 282 acres [114 hectares], so that the available space in the Necropolis is nearly seven times as large as that of all other like places of internment for metropolitan purposes put together.

The soil also is particularly suitable, combining all the conditions laid down by the Board of Health. It consists throughout of a light sandy soil, which insures the dryness so essential in ground devoted to internments; it has a broken and undulating surface, and may easily be made to possess the beauty upon which the Board of Health laid stress; and if the directors satisfy the public with regard to its "accessibility" and "cheapness of transit", they will have done much to establish the commercial success of their undertaking.

With regard to the cheapness of transit and the reduction upon the ordinary cost of burial the directors appeal to their scale of fees, for which they claim extreme moderation. Of course their hopes of cheapness of transit depended upon the disposition of the railway company, who, it is stated, have met them in the most liberal spirit.

At first there is to be a daily funeral train starting in the morning from the London terminus. Here a different reception and waiting room will be appropriated to each train of mourners and they will of course have private compartments in the railway carriage.

If necessary, however, the Necropolis Company undertake to conduct what may be termed the London portion of the funeral – namely the conveyance of the body from the residence of the deceased to the railway station, so that offices may, if it is wished, be placed in their hands, or in those of responsible undertakers with whom they have contracted.

The scale of charges given in the primed tariff of the company is £17.4s, £9.8s, £6 and £2.9s, the moderation of which is expected to have an important social bearing, inasmuch as it is an attempt to put an end to that barbarous practice of a large funeral expenditure from which the public at present suffer, and which they are little able to control.

Stamford Mercury, 17 November 1854

AGHAST AT PRENDERGAST'S MURDER BY COUSIN

A barbarous murder has been committed at Claremorris in the county of Mayo. The mutilated remains of respectable young man, James Prendergast, son of the toll-collector of the town, were discovered floating in the water of a stagnant pool, within a few 100 yards [94.11 metres] of the town.

The body presented a most horrible spectacle; the head being severed and tied in a bag, the thighs and legs also cut off, as it would appear, by a hatchet or some other blunt instrument. The hands were tied with strips of calico, to which were attached heavy stones, in order that the body might not float: but it did float.

The deceased had been missed for a month. He had saved money to convey him to America, and it is believed he was murdered and robbed by his own cousin. This person, named Maurice Prendergast, has been apprehended in an American ship in Liverpool, on board of which he had been conveyed in a trunk at the instigation of the woman who accompanied him.

Carlisle Journal, 4 January 1856

SUDS LAW – SOAP-MAKER'S SLIPPERY SLIDE TO OBLIVION

As M. Honhart, a soap manufacturer, at Colman, was, three mornings ago, standing on a stool to examine a vessel containing boiling liquid, the stool broke beneath his weight, and he fell into the mixture. Being unable to extricate himself, he was in a short time scalded to death.

The Ipswich Journal, 23 August 1856

SPONTANEOUS COMBUSTION FIRES
UP THE IMAGINATION

During the last few days public curiosity has been has been excited to a very unusual pitch by a series of occurrences... On Tuesday night, the 12th inst, an alarm of fire was raised, and, on proceeding to the scene of the danger, a house abutting on the large store-yard belonging to Messrs. Howard, the celebrated implement makers, and tenanted by one of their servants, was on fire.

It appeared that the family had taken the opportunity of the master's absence to have a good cleaning down, with an especial view to the riddance of a certain pest better known to Londoners than the happy dwellers in the country. In furtherance of the latter part of this truly housewifery design recourse was had to fumigation. A vessel containing broken roll sulphur was placed in what was deemed to be a safe position – viz. in a bassinette, which was removed from its usual place and set in the middle of the room. The sulphur was duly ignited, and the room of course vacated by all except the obnoxious vermin.

In the space of two hours it was discovered that the sulphurous fluid had escaped into the bassinette, had burnt through the bottom, fired the floor, and eaten its way through the planks. Timely observation and alarm railed to arrest the progress of the fire. All was deemed safe. But on Saturday evening the head of the family returned, and on retiring to rest, and having innocently thrown his damp stockings on the carpet, what was his astonishment at seeing them ignite! Something like a panic seized the household, but at length their fears were pacified and they went to rest.

On Sunday morning, while the master was attending Divine service at the Methodist chapel, fire was again discovered in the house. Considerable consternation was occasioned to the assembly by the calling out of a fireman during service, and also by the master's disappearance from his pew. These fires were suppressed, but in the course of the day no less than 30 fires broke out in different parts of the house – in the presence of visitors, most respectable and intelligent men.

Every part of the furniture in every room of the house appeared to be charged with some mysterious self-igniting gas. Smoke issued suddenly from cupboards, large and small, from almost every drawer, and even from boxes of linen and woollen materials which had not been opened for some length of time prior to Tuesday's fire.

Some of the statements made before the coroner are so startling as to be nearly incredible. One gentleman laid his handkerchief down upon the sofa when it forthwith ignited. Another gentleman, while discussing the marvels of the day and washing his hands, discovered that the damp towels on the horse in the bedroom were on fire.

A lady, anxious to prevent further mischief, had a short time previously examined a box containing articles appertaining to feminine apparel, and pronouncing it safe had shut it up, but on going to remove it felt that it was hot, and on re-opening it discovered the contents in a blaze. On Monday morning the phenomena, somewhat abated, re-appeared, and it was found that the greater part of the property in the house was charred or burnt to tinder.

Two medical gentlemen – Dr Barker and Mr Blower – visited the scene of the fiery mystery, and at noon made an application to the sitting magistrate (in the absence of the mayor) for sanction to their proposal of submitting the matter to the coroner. In the course of the prolonged enquiry the medical gentlemen were of the opinion that the sulphurous fumes, in connection with the gas of the charred wood, had charged the entire house with inflammable gas, which, in some cases by friction, in others by electricity, had been from time to time ignited. The verdict of the jury was, according to the evidence, so far as the fire was concerned, "Accidental", and with regard to the other fires the verdict was an open one.

IF ONLY HE'D ASKED FOR AN *EAU-DE-VIE* FRUIT BRANDY INSTEAD

The Rev. Thos. Marsh, a passenger by the steamer *Canadian* from Quebec, died a day or two before the arrival of the vessel at Liverpool, from a sad mis-chance. He asked for a mineral water, which the steward had not got; the steward brought him chloride of zinc in a basin, and Mr. Marsh drank some of it thinking it was medicinal water. Medical aid was in vain, and he died after much suffering.

NO COCK-AND-BULL STORY

On Monday morning a little girl lost her life through being gored by an infuriated bullock. At Rathbone Place [London] someone struck it with a whip, the effect which was that it became very wild. It ran away from the driver who had the charge of it. On its way it plunged one of its horns into the skull of a child named Paul, who was playing with some other children. The animal proceeded with the child into Charlotte Court, and there dropped it in front of the house where its parents resided, and where a quantity blood and brains dropped from the wound. The child was carried dead to Middlesex Hospital.

A MAN KILLED BY HIS OWN COFFIN

On Saturday night last a man, who resided in Twenty-ninth-street, was killed in a most singular manner. The following are the peculiar circumstances, so far as our reporter has been enabled to learn – for, in consequence of the opinion entertained concerning his relatives by the deceased, who was a man of considerable wealth and respectability, they have made a great effort to keep the particulars from the public ear.

It appears that nearly a year ago the deceased, who was 53 years of age, became strongly impressed with an idea that when he should die, the parsimonious disposition of his relatives would lead them to put him in a cheap coffin, while he had a strong desire to be put in one of polished rosewood, lined with white satin, and trimmed with silver.

Soon after this strange idea got possession of his mind, he discovered an elegant coffin in one of the principal warehouses which suited him. He purchased it for 75 dollars; had it sent to his residence at nightfall, and stowed it away in a small closet adjoining his bedroom, where it remained until the time of the accident.

How it occurred is not known to a certainty, for the first intimation the family had of the lamentable occurrence was from a servant, who, on going to call him to breakfast, found the door wide open and the deceased lying upon the floor dead, with his coffin at his side. She screamed, which soon brought the family, and on raising the body, the skull was found crushed in upon the brain.

When discovered, to all appearance, he had been dead several hours. On examining the closet, a bottle containing a quantity of sherry wine was found, and, as Saturday night was excessively warm, he is supposed to have gone to the closet in order to procure the wine to use with some ice water he had on a small table by his bedside. It is thought that he must have sought for it in the dark, and by some mistake upset the coffin, which stood nearly upright. Becoming sensible that it was falling, he probably made an effort to get away, when he fell, and the outer edge struck his head with sufficient force to fracture his skull and cause almost immediate death. *New York Paper*.

Worcestershire Chronicle, 30 November 1859

FOOD FOR THOUGHT – HOW TO AVOID GETTING IN A PICKLE

There is at present in the Bradford Infirmary a basket-maker, named Charles Sutton, who has been suffering from symptoms referable to poisoning by lead. He has lost the use of his hands, but is improving under treatment. After much fruitless inquiry as to the cause, it was found that the man had been wont to eat pork which had been pickled in a leaden cistern. It is said to be the practice of pork butchers at Bradford, and perhaps elsewhere, to pickle pork in such cisterns, under the idea that the process is thereby facilitated. The plan, however, is fraught with danger to life, as the lead is certain to be corroded by the salt.

SAILOR'S HAIR-RAISING EXPERIENCE

A few days since, while the express train from London to Exeter was going at the rate of 60 miles an hour, a sailor lost his cap just above the village of Stoke. He instantly opened the carriage door and sprung out after it. The guard who witnessed this was sure that Jack was killed but went to check just in case. Jack turned up shortly afterwards with only his arm broken. He went on to Plymouth the same night and appeared to be quite unconscious of the hairbreadth escape he had had.

Dunfermline Saturday Press, 10 August 1867

MAKING A MEAL OF THE WILDLIFE PERILS IN JAVA

We should fancy the people of Java must have a lively time of it. According to the latest official statistics contained in the *Tijdschrift vor Nederlavdsch Java*, the tiger has in one single year consumed exactly 148 human beings, and in another year 131. The crocodiles cleared an average of 50 people a year, while serpents accounted for between 22 and 43. But the Dutch seem to accept their fate with characteristic equanimity. The Governor-General, a long while ago, offered a prize for every tiger that was killed the munificent sum of guilders 22 (£2). His subjects apparently prefer being eaten by the tiger.

Illustrated Police News, 25 June 1870

DYING TO WEAR THE LATEST FASHION

It would be impossible to form anything like an accurate estimate of the thousands of persons who have fallen victim to the odious fashion of tight-lacing. A melancholy instance of this baneful practice occurred in New Town on Saturday last. Dorothea, the eldest daughter of Vincent Posthelwaite, Esq, (a highly respectable and wealthy merchant of New Town), died suddenly at a ball given in her father's house.

While dancing with a young gentleman to whom she was engaged, she was observed by her partner to turn pale and to gasp spasmodically for breath; she tottered for a few brief seconds, and then fell. The general impression was that she had fainted: restoratives were applied without producing the desired effect.

A doctor was sent for, who, upon examining the patient, pronounced the ill-fated young lady to be dead. The consternation of the family and guests may be readily imagined, which was not a little enhanced by the medical gentleman declaring that Miss Posthelwaite had died from no other cause than that of tight-lacing – the heart's action had been impeded, the excitement and exertion was, under the circumstances, too great a strain upon the system, and hence sudden death.

Paisley Herald and Renfrewshire Advertiser, 13 January 1872

ELEVATING THE STATUS OF THE DEAD

It is a painful thing to see a corpse carried to the grave in an ugly black box under a mourning coach. It shows a want of respect for the dead person, for the relatives sit comfortably cushioned in a snug carriage while the poor dead person is shoved into a vulgar box, within a few inches of the surface of the road, and under their feet. In dirty weather this horrid box is bespattered with mud. The Dublin Police Commissioners have abolished this disgraceful custom: they have issued regulations that no coffin or corpse shall be conveyed in any carriage or hearse constructed also for the conveyance of passengers.

Sheffield Evening Telegraph, 23 December 1887

DESERTED ISLAND GARRISON – OUT OF SIGHT, OUT OF MIND

It is not often that a Colonial Governor finds himself the object of prosecution for his treatment of the people committed to his charge. Today, however, *M.* Genouille, who until recently held the post of Governor of Senegal, was tried for the manslaughter of four unlucky blacks – whom he had despatched as caretakers of the Isle of Alcatras annexed during his administration – and subsequently died of starvation on this barren spot, no attempt having been made after months of waiting to renew their meagre supply of provisions.

It was a decidedly hard case for the blacks from the first. The natives of these benighted regions entertain the utmost horror of life on islands which they regard as haunted by ghosts and goblins and evil spirits of the most ferocious type. It was, therefore, with considerable misgiving that these unfortunate Negroes consented to undertake the duty required of them, but on the eve of the departure of the despatch boat from Alcatras they plucked up courage and assured the commander that they were proud and happy to serve France, and that they would do their best.

After the interval of about a month a visit was paid to the island, but five months then elapsed without any effort being made to revictual the occupants, and it was not till the middle of May this year that these unfortunate creatures who had last been seen alive in November received serious attention from the authorities.

Their bodies were found lying on the ground reduced to the condition of mere skeletons. All their provisions had long disappeared, nor a drop of water was to be seen – they had died of hunger and thirst!

At the trial today M. Genouille threw the responsibility at Captain Ferrat, affirming that he had instructed him to look after these poor men. M. Ferrat on his side declared he had discharged his duty until his removal from his post at the end of last year, but he maintained that it was for the Governor to give the order for the despatch boat. The commander had merely to remind him of the existence of the blacks. After the hearing of the witnesses the Public Prosecutor addressed the Court, asking it to condemn M. Genouille, while Maitre Leon Renault delivered eloquent speech for the defence Judgment.

NOT-SO-FRIENDLY NEIGHBOURS

Dreadful Massacre Masailand, Zanzibar. News has been received that the Masai tribe has experienced disaster hitherto unknown. The Arusha tribe at the base of Mount Meru enticed the Masai warriors of El Moran to Ugogo on a grand cow-lifting expedition, and when they were well away the Arushas fell on their settlements and massacred all the old women, and children, drove off 14,000 cattle, and burned the villages. On their return the Masai spent three days in lamentation, and then assembled in general congregation. The chief priest Matabien then sent them to enter upon a war, which is likely to last three years, and to the devastation of the country west of Kilimanjaro.

Dover Express, 23 January 1891

DOZY SOMNAMBULIST RESPONSIBLE FOR BOY'S DEATH

A young man of 16, who resided in Toulon, has just fallen victim to the superstitious credulity of his relatives. The lad fell ill the other day, and his parents, instead of sending for a doctor, addressed themselves to a female somnambulist, who professed to exercise mysterious curative powers. She gave them a so-called specific for the ailment from which their son was presumed to be suffering, the mixture being one of her own composition. It was duly administered to the patient, and 24 hours later the young man died in frightful agony. A post-mortem examination showed that his death was (a correspondent declares) directly due to the potion. The wonder-working somnambulist has been arrested.

Liverpool Echo, 8 July 1893

KISS OF DEATH

A melancholy occurrence is reported from Hale, a little village near Farnham, during the festivities in celebration of the Royal Wedding. A young man named Windibank, who was playing kiss-in-the-ring, having run after and kissed a girl, fell down and died in a few minutes. The incident caused much consternation amongst the villagers.

HEAVENLY RAPTURES OVER AN INVENTION FOR A SUICIDE MACHINE

"I have solved the problem, and future generations will bless my name," said the philosopher, and his face wore a look of mingled complacency and triumph. "What problem have you solved?," I asked.

"I've taken from death its sting, and the little invention I have here will make the act of dissolution a positive pleasure. My invention is founded on that king of forces, electricity, and in brief is this. The subject is tired of life, he is out of work, with no chance of employment: his sweetheart has forsaken him for a more favoured suitor: he has taken too much wine: and the future looks black to him. In short, he wants to die but is afraid. He comes to me, and for a small fee I put him in the way of taking the last journey with a foretaste of heaven.

You see here a common electric clock: then you see there are two wires, one from either side: the one leads to a powerful dynamo and through it can be sent any number of volts it is deemed necessary to ensure instantaneous death. This dynamo, of course, is hidden. In fact, anything which would be the least suggestive of unpleasant things is absolutely barred from – shall I call it, my suicide parlours?

The other wire leads to this bed in the corner. The bed itself is one of the most important pieces of the machinery. Our friend seeking oblivion comes to me. As you know, I am a physician by training. I make a careful examination of him and am able to tell to a minute how large a quantity of given narcotic will take to send him into unconsciousness in a given time. I give him this dose and he sets the clock for the given time. He takes his place on the bed. As he does so, mechanism is set in motion which reveals copies of the masterpieces of art, both painting and sculpture, that the sense of sight is delighted.

At the same time the most perfect automatic musical instruments obtainable discourse the sweetest music: phonographs which have been charged with the most entrancing songs of the best singers join the heavenly chorus. The sense of hearing is charmed. Invisible censors burn with the most delicate and subtle perfumes, satisfying at once the senses of taste and smell. As the patient sinks into unconsciousness, with every sense gratified, just when the power to feel is about to leave him, he can feel the sweet, warm breath of the woman for whose loss perhaps he has sought death on his face, and her lips pressed to his.

Then comes – what? I do not know. All I know is that there is no more waking, no more pain, no more sorrow. So far as mortal mind can know it is the end. I propose at once to interest philanthropists in my invention, and when you get tired of giving your valuable aid to getting out the greatest newspaper in the world I'll be in a position to aid you in your praiseworthy aim with neatness and despatch – for a small consideration of course."— *New York Herald*.

WHEN THE LIGHTS WENT OUT

A Rome correspondent telegraphs: On the Piazza Quirinal last evening, two electric light lamp-men lost their lives through a piece of almost incredible carelessness. One of the large lamps opposite the Palace suddenly went out. The lamp-man belonging to the district brought a ladder and had ascended, but scarcely touched the carbon when he fell to the ground from a height of some 16 feet [4.86 metres]. His companion, believing him to be seized with sudden illness, went up to his place, but also immediately fell.

Both men had neglected to use the simple mechanism at the base of the lamp post which interrupts the electric current when any repairs or manipulation are necessary. The men were conveyed to the hospital, but were both dead. The engineer of the society states that the orders given to the men as to the use of the insulator are most vigorous and the men are daily exercised in its use. The King telephoned to the hospital an inquiry about the unfortunate men.

Leeds Times, 22 August 1896

TINFOIL WOULD HAVE FOILED TRAGIC DAGGER STAGE DEATH

The tragedy in real life at the Novelty Theatre, London should serve as a warning to members of the theatrical profession. Why

William Moritz Franks, who was unfortunate enough to kill his fellow actor, Temple Edgecumbe Crezier, should have resorted to the use of a dangerous weapon in a mere play is beyond conception.

Just as well might the claim be put forward by theatrical managers that for the purposes of realistic display in a stage battle scene it is essential to use ball instead of blank cartridge. A harmless piece of wood covered with tinfoil would have answered far better than a real weapon, for the metallic covering would have served to reflect the light and convey a livelier impression to the spectators.

It is really marvellous that more accidents do not happen on the stage from the indiscriminate use of dangerous weapons. Unfortunately a bad lesson has been set to the lesser lights by such men as the late Charles Kean and Henry Irving, who, expert swordsmen, have carried their mimicry of actual strife with dangerous implements to such extreme that the slightest accident might have entailed very serious consequences. When the danger was foreseen Franks never should have used the dagger. He is greatly to be commiserated with, and the accident will, no doubt, cast a cloud over a promising future career.

A BRUSH WITH DEATH

Wm. Bray, who was employed as a fitter at the Brush Electrical Engineering Works at Loughborough, met with a fatal accident. The unfortunate man was a son of Mr. Richard Bray, newsagent, of Waterside, Lincoln, and according to a letter procured from a gentleman engaged at the Loughborough works was greatly liked by his fellow workmen. It appears that Bray got caught on his lathe, and had his head cut off, death, of course, being instantaneous. Mr. Bray was at once telegraphed for, and went to Loughborough at once, the telegram informing him that his son had met with an accident.

Hull Daily Mail, 15 July 1901

HARD TO SWALLOW STORY BUT FALSE TEETH PROVED FATAL

Swallowing her false teeth, the wife of a Liverpool joiner died after an operation for their removal.

PRIVILEGED!

A man knocked a woman down in Matthias Road, Stoke Newington, on Saturday, and proceeded to jump on her. "It's all right; she's my wife," he remarked to policemen who came up. The unfortunate woman's condition is serious.

Evening Telegraph, 15 December 1908

MAKING WINING AND DINING AN ELECTRIFYING EXPERIENCE

Of the uses of electricity there is certainly no end [as exhibited at *The Modern Home Exhibition* at Cheltenham Town Hall]. One of its latest applications has taken the form of an addition to the smart dinner table in the shape of an electric tablecloth – a device of which up-to-date hostesses will not be long in taking advantage. The new tablecloth looks harmless enough – a simple sheet of grey felt, overlaid with ordinary damask tablecloth. Silver candlesticks are placed on the table – an unusual brilliance streaming from their dainty shades, and the uninitiated may wonder how candles can produce such dazzling light. But there is more in it than meets the eye, for running down the sides of each candlestick is an almost invisible wire with a tiny pronged end. This prong fastens itself into the tablecloth, and as it touches the cloth, the electric connection is complete, and the electric candles are lighted. Wherever the candlesticks are placed, as soon the prong touches the electric cloth, a brilliant light streams forth.

Essex Newsman, 20 August 1910

A MISTAKEN CASE OF "NO GRAIN, NO GAIN"?

A medical man stated at an inquest in Birkenhead that many girls ate raw rice to improve the complexion. The deceased girl, it was stated, had an inordinate appetite for raw rice, and this had a good deal to do with her death.

Exeter and Plymouth Gazette, 14 July 1930

SIR ARTHUR CONAN DOYLE –
HIS (VERY OWN) *LAST BOW!*

At a Spiritualist memorial service for Sir Arthur Conan Doyle at the Albert Hall last night, Mrs. Estelle Roberts, who for half an hour gave spirit descriptions and messages, ceased abruptly and turned, saying: "I have a message from him." She walked to Lady Conan Doyle and her family and engaged in apparently cheerful conversation.

Mrs. Roberts afterwards told a reporter: "I received a message from Sir Arthur himself, and I gave it to the family. It was a message to Lady Conan Doyle and her family, especially one of them." Lady Doyle said: "I am perfectly convinced that the message is from my husband. It is a happy message – one that is cheering and encouraging." Eight thousand people attended the service. An empty chair, with a slip bearing Sir Arthur's name, was next to Lady Doyle; but Mr. George Craze made it clear that any impression that Sir Arthur's materialised form was expected was quite erroneous.

MEDICAL ODDITIES,
QUACKS AND CURES

RAMMING IT HOME WHILST FEELING SHEEPISH ABOUT THE FAIRER SEX

Within the last few years a cruel disease hath robbed the fairer sex of their charms. This distemper is epidemical: it was imported from France, like another which shall be nameless [syphilis]; and appeared first among the Court ladies; it then seized the citizens' wives and daughters; and now it begins to make dreadful ravages in the country.

It affects the head in a strange manner: insomuch that, from a moderate and beautiful form, proportioned to the delicate body of a fine lady, it swells all at once to an enormous size; and I have known some females, four feet [1.2 metres] odd in height, go into their dressing rooms with heads not much larger than those of pins, and come out with Patagonian pericraniums [connective tissue membrane that surrounds the skull].

The tumour appears principally in the occiput [back of the head], and is so prodigious as to make the patient totter under the weight of it, and when the disease has been of long continuance, it generally produces a violent itching in the head.

The French call it *Tête de Mouton* [Mutton Head] because it makes the patient look like a ram. Some time after the head is swollen to a monstrous magnitude, it sends forth a foetid smell, and generally breeds vermin, which, I suppose, is not very wonderful, the maggots, which were first in the inside of the head, afterwards appearing outwardly.

LOVESICK OR JUST SICK?

Advertisement: *Dr. Henry's Chemical Nervous Medicine.* The many virtues of which are too well known to need repetition, their success being well attested by numberless persons, who, from a miserable languishing state, both of body and mind, have quickly been restored to health and quiet, by taking a few doses.

They never fail of giving relief in all nervous complaints such as hypochondriac melancholy, hysteric vapours, languors, palpitations, and trembling of the heart, giddiness, violent head-aches, noise in the ears, mists before the eyes, swimming of the head, fainting, lowness of spirits, obstructions in the capillary vessels, weakness of the brain, flushing in the face, irregular thoughts, agitation in the stomach or bowels: in short all disorders proceeding from wind and indigestion. And it is likewise of peculiar service in strengthening the nerves, removing all obstructions, and promoting a free circulation.

This excellent medicine is still prepared and sold at the Doctor's House in Hatton Garden, at 7 shillings the pint bottle, with a box of pills, and a paper of Cephalic Snuff for the immediate relief of all disorders of the head.

Newcastle Courant, 9 August 1806

BUGGED BY NIGHTMARE BED BUGS

Opthalmia. The 28th Regiment of Foot and the Herefordshire militia removed on Monday last from Colchester, in consequence of this sudden and afflicting disorder having attacked numbers of both regiments, to Maldon ... A medical board has attended to investigate ... to quiet the anxiety of the neighbourhood as to its being epidemic.

The report of the result has not been made but it was considered to have originated in the bed-clothes brought over by the 28th and other regiments from Egypt, being used this season, which, when exposed to the heat of the weather, engendered a small insect, and the sleeping-rooms of the men being close, many who went to bed well in their eye-sight, were awoke in the morning with an inflammation, feeling as if some fire sand had got into them and, notwithstanding every assistance, a number of men of both regiments are totally blind.

Kendal Mercury, 17 March 1838

SOLUTION FOR SEAMEN SAILING TOO CLOSE
TO THE WIND WHILST STATIONED IN PORT

Advertisement: *Yoland's Specific Solution,* for the cure of gonorrhoea, gleets [discharge], strictures, irritation of the kidneys, bladder, urethra, prostate gland, and all diseases of the urinary organs. It is offered to the public upon the authority and recommendation of several medical men of the highest standing in the profession, and is warranted to cure the above diseases in much shorter space of time than any medicine that has ever been prepared or sold in this country. In addition to which it is agreeable to the palate, and invariably improves the constitution however much it may have been impaired by disease, or by those injurious remedies, mercury, copaiba, turpentine, balsams, etc. *Yoland's Specific Solution* is now universally kept and prescribed at several of our principal hospitals, a fact which speaks volumes in its favour. One bottle having more effect than four of any other remedy for the cure of any of the above diseases.

Captains and seamen should make a point of taking a few bottles with them, as it is utterly impossible to procure any medicine that will effect half so quick and certain a cure.

The Cork Examiner, 22 April 1842

IT'S OK TO BE BIG-HEADED ABOUT
BEING A CLASS-ACT IN LONDON

The majority of the heads of the higher classes in London are above the medium dimensions, whilst among the lower classes it is very hard to find a large head.

The Royal Leamington Spa Courier, 18 September 1847

WAS PIFFADY'S MIRACLE CURE JUST PIFFLE OR WAS IT A GRAVE MISTAKE?

A person named Piffady died lately at St.-Martin-du-Mont, aged 91, whose early life was marked by a curious circumstance. When about 30 years of age, and in the army, he was taken ill at Lille, and to all appearances expired in the hospital of that town. He was taken to the burial ground in the usual way, and was on the point of being consigned to the grave, when the volley fired by his comrades over his coffin roused him all at once from his lethargy, and caused him to strike against the wood loud enough to attract notice. The lid was raised at once, and Piffady stood forth on the burial ground, before the eyes of his astonished comrades. What was also curious is that he found himself cured of his illness by the sudden shock his system had received.

Sherborne and Yeovil Mercury, 11 March 1848

HOW DOCTORS WORM THEIR WAY INTO THEIR PATIENTS' AFFECTIONS

Advertisement: *Lamb's Vegetable Compound.* An effectual cure for all descriptions of worms that infest the human body, indigestion in all its varied forms, nervous diseases, bilious or liver complaints, all cases of fits arising from intestinal irritation, impurities of the blood, early stages of consumption, and all other ailments producing a delicate state of the constitution. Females of the most delicate constitution, either suckling or during pregnancy; young children, or persons at an advanced period of life, may take it with perfect safety, without hindrance of business or change of diet, and at all seasons of the year without the least danger of taking cold, and warranted not to contain any preparation of mercury or turpentine.

14 January 1848 – Mrs. Stringer, widow, monthly nurse, living

at Langdon's Cottage, near Bathwick Bridge, Bath, while under our treatment passed a tape-worm several yards [0.9 metres] long, with upwards of half a pint [0.28 litres] in small pieces. The symptoms that affected her for upwards of eight years were as follows: pain and giddiness in the head, with dimness of sight and heaviness over the eyes, bad taste in the mouth in the morning, a sensation of something rising in the throat with retchings to vomit, the food appearing to produce nothing but wind in the bowels, frequently violent gnawing pains, together with weakness between the stomach and bowels, aching pains in the limbs, pains in the back and sides, and scarcely ever felt refreshed from food or sleep. The worm may be seen by applying to Mr. Lamb.

Mrs. Hussey, of 85, Thomas Street, Bristol, while under our treatment passed a tape worm, upwards of eight yards [7.3 metres] long and half an inch [1.27cms] wide. The worm may be seen by applying to Mrs Hussey.

Bath Chronicle and Weekly Gazette, 24 April 1851

WIFE'S CHILDISH SATISFACTION IN KEEPING IN WITH AN INN-KEEPER

There is now residing at Waterford, Hertfordshire, the wife of a respectable licensed victualler, not more than 43 years age, who was safely delivered, on Monday week, of her 30th child.

Hereford Journal, 5 August 1857

PORES FOR THOUGHT – A CORNY CURE-ALL BUT SOFT ONES ONLY!

Advertisement: *Holloway's Ointment*. A medical revolution! The world unanimous. The virtue of disease often works its way through to the internal organs via the pores of the skin. This penetrating ointment, melting under the hand as it is rubbed in, is absorbed through the same channels, and reaching the seat of inflammation, promptly and invariably subdues it, whether located in the kidneys, liver, lungs or any other important organ. It penetrates the surface to the interior, through the countless tubes that communicate with the skin as summer rain passes into the fevered earth, diffusing its cold and regenerative influence. Both ointment and pills should be used in the case of "bad legs, bad breasts, sand fly and mosquito bites, sore nipples, cancers, piles, tumours, lumbago, fistulas, elephantiasis, scurvy, sore throats, scalds and corns (*soft*)".

Bucks Herald, 22 August 1857

HAIR-RAISING EXHIBITIONISM

A very extraordinary being, named Julia Pastrana, is now on exhibition at the Regent Gallery, London. With the exception of her head, she is in every respect a perfect woman, extremely well formed, with very small hands and feet, but arms somewhat short. Her height is about four feet six inches [1.37 metres], although her bust, which is well developed, is large enough for a female above the ordinary stature.

Her arms are thickly covered with long, silky, black hair, on the first phalange of her fingers, and to some extent so is the dorsum of the hands. The whole of her face is clothed more or less with hair, jet black, fine as silk, and perfectly straight. The facial angle is much like that of the Negro, but more acute, owing to the greater prominence of the jaw. This undue prominence is attributable to an extraordinary thickening of the front of the alveolar border of the upper jaw, causing the lips to turn outwards, and a kind of hard wart-like growth of the lower gum.

In these processes she has no front teeth. These grow in what may be styled inner gums. Here the lower set is perfect, but in the upper set the front teeth are almost deficient, though on close examination one or two may be perceived embedded in the jaw. The tongue is large and thick, and presents the appearance of a spongy mass.

Her ears are very much elongated, somewhat narrow, and thickly covered with long hair. Her forehead is low and retreating, and the skin, instead of being thin and smooth, is extremely thick and hairy, but there is a perceptible difference between the texture of the hair on this part of the face, and that of the head.

The nose is destitute of cartilage, and the wings of it are very much flattened and expanded. Her eyes are deeply set and quite black, and the pupils appear to dilate only very slightly under the strongest light. Their expression is pleasing, and somewhat mournful. Eyebrows are distinctly marked, being very wide and thick and meeting in front, seeming to form a band of hair on the brow.

The whole of the face is thickly covered with hair, which increases in length and thickness as it approaches the sides of the cheeks and the chin, under from which it depends to perhaps nearly two inches [5 cms] in length. The skin is of copper colour, and very delicate.

Julia Pastrana is full of intelligence, highly sensitive, the kindest disposition, witty to a surprising degree, and though not educated appears to be extremely apt at learning, for she sings English and Spanish ballads with considerable expression, her voice being quite feminine. She is now 23 years of age. Her mother is said to have been a Mexican root-digger Indian, and was captured by a *ranchero* in the Sierra Madre, whence she was conveyed to Governor Sanchez, of Sinaloa, in whose house she died when Julia was two years old.

HEAR! HEAR! SOUNDS JUST LIKE HEARSAY

Advertisement: Dr John Nichol Watters, 32, Spring Gardens, Charing Cross, cured himself of nine years' deafness and distressing noises by an expeditious and simple treatment discovered during a residence in China, also hundreds of private patients incurably deaf. By this book deafness need no more be dreaded – sufferers can cure themselves – explaining how the author was cured, the means used, hundreds of startling cures published, rescuing the deaf from snares and frauds of daily advertising quacks, pretended consulting surgeons to institutions, etc.

Eminent physicians and clergymen, some of whom have been cured by Dr. Watters, can honestly and truly testify the fact, having witnessed with startling amazement deaf children and aged sufferers made to hear conversation perfectly, although deaf for 40 or 50 years. Dr. Watters is a Member of the Royal English College of Surgeons, obtained his Diploma, March 31, 1843, also Licentiate of the London Royal Apothecaries' Hall, Diploma granted January 30, 1830. By one consultation he guarantees to restore hearing, however incredible it appears, without an instant's inconvenience or suffering.

VENERABLE SUCCESS FOR VENEREAL EXCESS

Advertisement: *Cordial balm of Syriacum* is expressly employed to renovate the impaired powers of life, when exhausted by the influence exerted by solitary indulgence on the system. Its action is purely balsamic; its power in re-invigorating the frame in all cases of nervous and sexual debility, impotency, barrenness, and debilities arising from venereal excesses, has been demonstrated by its unvarying success in thousands of cases. To those persons who are prevented from entering the married state in consequence of early errors, it is invaluable.

Dunfermline Saturday Press, 10 August 1867

SCIENTIFIC INFANTICIDE BY DOCTOR USING LAUDED INVENTOR'S FORMULA

[Justus von Liebig, the chemist who discovered the use of nitrogen as an essential plant nutrient, also developed a manufacturing process for beef extracts and founded the Liebig Extract of Meat Company that later trademarked the *Oxo* stock cube. He is also known as the inventor of *Marmite* due to his discovery that yeast could be concentrated.]

Baron Liebig, whose fertile invention is always at work, has discovered what he deems a good substitute for maternal milk. It is composed of cows' milk, flour, malt, and lactate and butyrate or carbonate of potassa. This looks as if it must be rather an abominable compound. At a recent meeting of the Paris Academy of Medicine this invention was discussed and condemned. Dr Depaul said that he had tried a series of experiments with it, conducting them with the utmost exactitude according to the inventor's directions.

"The first two children he tried it on were twins, born somewhat before the time. They weighed less than the average of new-born infants. Liebig's compound being administered to them instead of milk, they both died in the course of two days. A third infant, apparently in perfect health and above the average weight, died on the third day after taking the compound; and a fourth child, also healthy, died on the fourth day. In consequence of this he did not consider it advisable to continue his experiments."

We should rather think not. Here are four children coolly murdered in a scientific manner, and the operator expresses no regret, but simply says that it is perhaps better not to go on.

Leeds Times, 18 October 1873

NOSEY PEOPLE WELCOMED AT
THE NO-NOSE CLUB

Miss Sanborn tells us that an eccentric gentleman, having taken a fancy to see a large party of nose-less persons [as a consequence of syphilis], invited every one thus afflicted, whom he met in the streets, to dine on a certain day at a tavern, where he formed them into a brotherhood. He ordered a plentiful dinner, and told the landlord who were to be his guests, so that he might be a little prepared for their appearance.

No sooner was the hand of Covent Garden dial upon the stroke of the hour appointed than the No-Nose company began to drop in, asking for Mr. Crampton, which was the feigned name of their host, and succeeding one another so thickly that the waiter could scarcely show one up the stairs before he had another to conduct.

As the number increased, the surprise grew all the greater among those that were present, who stared at one another with unaccustomed bashfulness and confused oddness, as if every sinner beheld his own iniquities in the faces of his companions. Wine was called for, and generously furnished, with the simple restriction of the forfeiture of a quart if anyone should presume to put his nose in the glass. This club met every month for a whole joyous year, when its founder died, and the flat-faced community were unhappily dissolved.

Edinburgh Evening News, 19 April 1886

WAS HER GOAL TO HAVE HER
OWN FOOTBALL TEAM?

At Distington, near Workington, the wife of an artisan has just been delivered of triplets. The remarkable feature in the history of the married life of this lady is that it is only 11 months since she gave birth to triplets before, and previous to that she had twins twice, thus being the mother of 10 children in very little more than four years.

A BRAINY SOLUTION HOPED FOR BY
PATIENTS OF PASTEUR

A mad donkey at Menton, [France] has just provided [chemist and biologist] *M.* [Louis] Pasteur with two new patients. The animal, which had itself been bitten by a mad dog, attacked its owner and a veterinary surgeon who came to treat it, inflicting severe bites on them both; and they both started immediately for Paris, bringing with them the brains of the ass which had done the mischief.

They are not the only sufferers by the accident, which has cast slur, in local estimation at least, on the whole family of quadrupeds to which the offending animal belongs. The mountain excursions on donkey-back, which visitors to those parts were in the habit of indulging, have fallen into temporary disfavour; and the donkey-boys have been heavy losers by the lull in their industry.

Liverpool Echo, 8 July 1893

MOTHER'S AIRY-FAIRY DEFENCE OF EXHIBITING
THE "BALLOON-HEADED" BABY

There has been on exhibition in Leeds these past few weeks a baby with a head of extraordinary proportions, and its inspection by several medical gentlemen led to prosecution before the stipendiary magistrate (Mr. Bruce) yesterday afternoon. The child had previously been shown in Birmingham, Sheffield, London, Leicester, Newcastle, and elsewhere, when the local inspector for the prevention of cruelty to children took the case. Tom Norman, a show man, living in Merrion Street, and Jane Charrington, the mother of the child, were the defendants. It was proved that the infant bad been shown as "the balloon-headed baby" at a charge of 1d. Two medical gentlemen swore that the child was suffering from water on the brain, and that it being exhibited was an act of cruelty. For the defence two doctors were called to prove that there was no cruelty. Mr. Bruce decided to convict and fine Norman £5, and Charrington £1.

Illustrated Police News, 29 August 1896

LIVING LIFE TO THE FULL ALL IN EIGHT MONTHS

Marvellous Freak Of Nature In An Eight Months' Old Baby. There died on Monday in St. Louis, says a Daily Mail correspondent, the most extraordinary case of *lusus naturae* [deformed person] that has probably ever been known. Herman Bench was eight months old at his death, which was caused, the doctors say, through senile decay.

Imagine the strange course of nature that in eight months converts the baby into the decrepit man of 80. This individual – it can scarcely be called a child – had a fully developed head, its face had the aspect of maturity, and on it age had placed the lines of care. During its brief existence it grew a beard and manifested other signs of maturity. Lastly, with respect to intelligence, it passed through all the mental stages peculiar to mankind, from prattling babyhood to youthful volubility, and from middle-aged meditativeness to senile garrulity and then to extinction. All this in eight months.

Hereford Times, 13 November 1909

EYE SAY – RAPID CURE IN THE BLINK OF AN EYE

Advertisement: Why children blink. The notable increase in eye disease throughout the public schools, says a specialist, is chiefly the neglect of the parents. The constant blinking of the eyes is due to nervousness, and unless checked, becomes a real affliction. Children who blink constantly when spoken to enlarge the tiny muscles of the eyelids and set up an irritation which eventually affects the sight. The truth of this is apparent to anyone who watches a nervous child.

How easily this nervousness may be nipped in the bud by a judicious administration of *Phosferine* is evidenced by the testimony of Mrs. Peter Hazzard who says: "My children were so nervous and afraid of the dark, they would scream and cling to anyone, but thanks to *Phosferine* their nerves are stronger and they are not afraid to go anywhere by themselves now."

CARPING CRITICS
AND CRITICAL ISSUES OF THE DAY

Oxford Journal, 5 May 1753

WHY LADIES SHOULD BE CHASTE IN ORDER TO BE CHASED

Advertisement: This day was published (price bound 1 shilling) a new edition, corrected, of *The Whole Duty of Woman*, by A Lady. Written by the desire of A Noble Lord. Under the following headings: Curiosity, Censure, Acquaintance, Marriage, Reflection, Insinuation, Friendship, Education, Vanity, Affectation, Elegance, Authority, Knowledge, Modesty, Frugality, Widowhood, Reputation, Chastity, Employment, Religion, Complacence, Virginity. Printed for R. Baldwin in Paternoster Row.

The London Magazine, or *Gentlemen's Monthly Intelligencer*, January 1768

WORLD EXCLUSIVE! THE MAN TO BLAME FOR HOTEL AND RESTAURANT SERVICE CHARGES?

To the Author

Sir

Beggars having been ever deemed nuisances, disgraceful to Christianity and even common society; and although at gentlemen's houses their servants do not actually beg, yet is their acceptance of a gratuity beggarly, and the person who offers it must be himself of a mean spirit, as he thereby offers a gross affront to the master of the house. These beggars of the dumb class, although probably beggars bred, yet should not be suffered to bring their itch into a family. But they are the beggars of another tribe I am about to speak of, bred and licensed beggars, which you meet at every inn, when no sooner is the bill called for, but the setters prick up their ears, and scamper to obstruct the avenues of retreat.

The appearance, in the way to your horse and carriage, of everyone concerned to deliver what you have ordered, give significant intimations of their demands upon you, which, if you neglect, you will be sure to hear them bawl out with an insolent tone of petition, as: 'Pray remember the ostler', 'pray remember the waiter', 'pray remember the chambermaid', 'pray remember the boot-catcher', etc. And if you could insensibly pass the gauntlet, you must also pass that of their scurrilous abuse, as, 'You are no gentleman', and 'probably a scrub', or 'a scoundrel', and all this while, perhaps, the landlord or landlady present, quite unconcerned, wishing you a very good journey. They have got their demands and their servants are at liberty to bully you for their wages.

Such is the present scandalous situation at the inns in England, owing to the wretched state of their unprovided servants, who frequently suffer for their masters ill-usage; unprovided, because the generality coming from the dunghill and sturdy beggars bred, are suffered to continue so, through the mean greediness of their masters, who thereby merit no better guests than gamblers.

Now, find all the advertisements of new inn-keepers, their offerings of the best accommodation, and most genteel treatments: I would put them in a certain method to perform these offers in the most agreeable manner for their guests, and most useful to themselves. For which purpose I propose they should retain no beggars, but provide sufficiently for their servants, without allowing them to accept any perquisites at all. Now the question arises, 'how must the desired reformation be accomplished consistent with reciprocal advantage'? I answer, that allowing the established custom of some acknowledgement for attendance at inns, let the landlords pay their servants sufficient wages, and at the bottom of the bill, write attendance, leaving a blank for the person to give what he pleases; for every traveller would prefer the method of having only one person to pay... you will find it much easier to make the landlord an allowance for that purpose, than to cram the hungry jaws of his gaping cormorants, who are so irregularly fed. R.W.

Leeds Intelligencer, 5 July 1768

WAXING LYRICAL ABOUT MAKING DUMMIES OUT OF STUFFED-SHIRT GOVERNMENT MINISTERS

Letter to the Publisher: We have been told of a German Prince of final revenues and dominion, who, to preserve his dignity, and not overburden his subjects with taxes, nor to make them uneasy with any suspicion of a design against their liberties, had his army of 40 men in wax, who were exercised by clock-work. These served the purpose of state and showed as well as so many men of flesh and blood, and saved a great deal of expense. A project which I have formed, taken from the wisdom of a German Prince, is, in all the departments of the state, to have ministers made of wax.

The benefits cannot all be enumerated in this letter; but I shall just mention the vast and inconceivable saving to the public from their salaries, and places and pensions, which would reduce the national debt in a few years, within a moderate degree, and enable us to lessen some and annihilate other taxes.

I presume nobody will pretend to say that a waxen ministry will not do the business of the nation full as well as those we have. For I remember to have heard Mr. [Henry] Pelham say, when he was at the head of the administration [Prime Minister], that the public business was done by the secretaries and clerks in offices, at the salaries of 50 pounds and 100 pounds a year.

The ministry we have at present are soft and pliable to any impression which the master of the show will please to make... they seem to be playing at the game which children call "Make believe;" for nobody can suppose they are in earnest in the fantastical movements that they are making every day. An Englishman.

Cambridge Chronicle and Journal, 1 January 1813

THE WORLD'S MOST BORING BOOK AND BOOK TITLE?

The Annals of Literature, fertile in curiosities and calamities, have preserved few anecdotes more remarkable than that of our own times, which we are about to record: The Rev. William Davy, curate of Lustleigh in Devonshire, finished in the year 1807, a work of which the title will be a sufficient sample:

"A System of Divinity, in a course of sermons on the First Institutions of religion; on the Being and Attributes of God; on some of the most important Articles of the Christian Religion in connection; and on the several Virtues and Vices of Mankind, with occasional discourses. Being a compilation from the best sentiments of the polite writers and eminent sound divines, both ancient and modern, on the same subjects, properly connected, with improvements; particularly adapted for the use of chief families, and students in divinity, for churches and for the benefit of mankind in general."

The history of this work, which extends to 26 volumes, is a surprising and mournful case of wasted perseverance. Mr. Davy attempted to publish his collection by subscription: this he found did not answer; so he stopped short, and resolved to print it himself – that is, with his own hands. He was poor, and for a reason which is sufficiently apparent, his theological labours could obtain no patronage; but his ardour and invincible patience overcame all difficulties. He purchased many worn out and cast-off types from a country printing-office as sufficed him to set up two pages; the outlay could not be more than the value of the metal, and he made a press for himself.

With these materials he went to work in the year 1795: performing every operation himself, and working off page by page, he struck off 40 copies of the first 300 pages; 26 of which he distributed among the universities, the bishops, the Royal Society and the reviews, hoping, no doubt, to receive from some of those quarters the encouragement which he thought himself entitled.

Disappointed in this, he resolved to spare himself any further expense of paper upon those before whom he had thrown his pearls in vain; and as he had reserved only 14 copies of the 40 with which commenced he continued to print, and at the end of 12 years of unremitting toil, finished the whole 26 volumes. This is a tale which excites respect for the amazing perseverance of the patient labourer, as well as compassion for its misdirection.

The Examiner, 28 August 1836

CLAWS FOR THOUGHT – EAT YOUR HEART OUT DOROTHY PARKER

Memorials of Mrs Hemans. With *Illustrations of her Literary Character from her Private Correspondence*. By Henry F. Chorley, In 2 vols., Saunders and Otley. 1836. This is an amiable and inoffensive book, but we cannot exactly see why it should have been published. We do not find any illustrations of a distinct literary character in the correspondence of Mrs Hemans. Her letters are of no mark – any schoolgirl would write as well. Her public career has not a particle of interest in it, and if her private life contained any, Mr Chorley has purposely withheld it. No doubt he had excellent reasons for doing so.

Woolmer's Exeter and Plymouth Gazette, 27 August 1842

THIS ED'S A GREEN-EYED MONSTER LACKING GRACE IN ANY SHAPE OR FORM

[In 1838 the steamship Forfarshire suffered engine failure, floundered, and broke in half in a fierce storm off the coast of

Northumberland. Grace Darling, 19, and her lighthouse-keeper father used a small rowing boat in treacherous sea conditions to save the lives of nine people. They were awarded several medals, Queen Victoria sent Grace £50, and the ensuing public accolade included a poem by William Wordsworth enshrining Grace's memory.]

Several of the papers say Grace Darling, the heroine of the Farne Islands, is in very bad health. She is at present on the main land for a change of air; and although reported to be somewhat better since she took up her residence there, she still looks very unwell.

(We wonder our contemporaries do not know better than to suppose that the public generally are interested in the health of this peasant. They could but publish such particulars of Victoria, the Grace and Darling of Great Britain, in whose health and looks every subject of her realm is indeed interested. —Ed.)

Dundee Courier, 22 October 1844

FALSE FLATTERY SOON FLATTENS THE EGO

The editor of a Newark paper recently published what he took for a very poetical effusion, sent to him from some amateur poet. On looking at the matter, after it was printed in his paper with complimentary remarks, he discovered that it was an acrostic upon his own name, in which he was likened to a jackass.

Hereford Journal, 5 August 1857, reproducing an article in *The Lancet*

SHAMEFULLY DOCTORING GENDER RESULTS

Miss Jessie Meriton White, a strong-minded lady of very pronounced political opinions, who was recently lecturing in England on Italian emancipation, has been so unfortunate as to get into prison at Genoa for interfering with politics, and has had the further mischance to find a champion in a certain George Morant, Junior. Writing from Carrickmacross to contradict the description of her arrest given by *The Times's* correspondent, this knight aberrant becomes quite ecstatic as to the lady's high intellect and great philanthropy.

He informs the public that politics had nothing to do with Miss White's mission, but that she, with moral courage worthy of all praise, after having endeavoured in vain to obtain an entrance into the medical and surgical institutions of England with a view to obtaining her diploma, in imitation of the Misses, Blackwell [Elizabeth Blackwell was the first woman to receive a medical degree in the USA, and sister Emily was the third] and others, proceeded to Italy, in the expectation of there meeting with liberality in the acquirement of the requisite professional knowledge which she had been denied in England.

If such really was the expectation of this poor deluded gentlewoman she must have been terribly hoaxed: but let that pass. We hold that the refusal of the British medical schools to receive her as a pupil was wisely resolved. We trust that the same course will be pursued wherever woman, who fancies herself qualified for an M.D. because she has a bee in her bonnet, seeks to enrol herself as a medical studentess; and to assume the academic cap and gown, far less becoming than the female articles of attire bearing the same names.

We can fancy the outcry amongst the horror-stricken teachers and damsels, "fluttered like doves," were any medical student with a nice taste for worsted work, or natural genius for crochet, to claim right of attendance on the lectures at any college for young ladies. If there be any earnest and perfectly sane women who entertain the opinion that medicine is their mission, let them start colleges of their own.

Belfast Morning News, 27 November 1857

IS THERE A CURE FOR DOCTORS' BAD HAND-WRITING?

A curious case was heard in the City of London Sheriffs' Court, on the 11th, which shows how necessary it is for professional men to write legibly. A person named English applied, in October 1854, to be admitted as a member of a certain benefit society, entitled *The Confident Fire and Life Assurance Company and Loan Office* but, as the medical officer, Dr. Jones, pronounced the applicant unhealthy, his proposal was rejected.

A week or so afterwards, English made a second application, and was then admitted, although at this time he was suffering from a serious affection of the lungs. Afterwards he contributed 17s 6d to the society, then declared upon the funds, and was allowed to draw about £14.

An inquiry, however, took place, and it was discovered that he had been admitted through a curious blunder, for which the doctor was properly responsible. The medical certificate described English as *not* fit for membership, but the important little word was written so indistinctly that it got corrupted into *now*.

The managers of the society grew impatient with the mistake and its burden, and refused to continue Mr. English's allowance, whereupon he brought an action against them. The judge said that Dr. Jones's writing was so indistinct that it would justify either reading but, as the plaintiff had signed a declaration that he had not suffered any illness for three and a half years, a verdict for the defendant was given and the judge naively remarked that, "if doctors would write legibly, a world of trouble would be saved."

Bath Chronicle and Weekly Gazette, 4 October 1866

CHAPTER AND VERSE ON BRINGING A QUICK END TO THIS THIEF OF TIME

The Pall Mall Gazette, reviewing Captain Mayne Reid's story of *The Bandolero*, says the right way to read it – "assuming that is to be read at all – is to begin at page 306, the number of pages in the book being 308, and continue until you have had enough of it. A considerable part of page 307 may be omitted with advantage, but this is perhaps hypercriticism."

Bradford Daily Telegraph, 9 January 1875

PUFFER TRAIN ON THE MET LINE

I have lately had the opportunity of ascertaining how the working classes use the cheap workmen's trains on the Metropolitan Railway which run between 5 and 6am. Any of those trains is quite a sight. It is packed full of working men in their working dress. Not only is every seat of the third-class carriage full, but the men stand up in a row between the seats. They all smoke away like so many Lancashire chimney stacks, and as the stuff they burn is of the vilest quality, the stench is something fearsome. The doors of the first-class carriages are carefully locked, so that the malodorous wearers of fustian may not get in, and are open only in the rare event of there being a first-class passenger.

Western Daily Press, 23 April 1878

WHAT THE DICKENS IS GOING ON HERE?

Charles Dickens' *The Vacant Chair* [*The Empty Chair* by Samuel Luke Fildes] was sold last week for 31 guineas. Its original price was 16 shillings. The sale was that of the effects of the late Edward Wilson, the well-known Australian newspaper proprietor. He purchased *The Vacant [Empty] Chair*, with several small odds and ends, at the Dickens' sale, at Gadshill [Dickens' residence], for £200.

Last week the entire lot realised only £39. This does not imply that Dickens' literary popularity has decreased, but we fear it does mean that the John Forster [critic and friend of Charles Dickens] biography has done its work, and that the personal prestige of the great novelist has greatly decreased.

Aberdeen Evening Express, 20 January 1879

FOOD FOR THOUGHT – TURNER'S EGGS AND SPINACH

Turner's Eccentricities. I used to meet [JMW] Turner at the table of Mr [John James] Ruskin, the father of the art critic [John]. The first occasion was a few days after the appearance of a notice in the *Athenaeum*, of a picture of Turner's, which was therein characterised as "eggs and spinach". This stuck in the great painter's throat, and as we were returning together, in Mr Ruskin's carriage, Turner ejaculated the obnoxious phrase every five minutes. I told him that, if I had attained to his eminence in art, I should not care a rush for what anyone said of me. But the only reply I could get was "eggs and spinach".

I was told, on very good authority, that Turner, whose economical habits were patent to all who knew him, had his dinner daily from a cook-shop; and it would sometimes happen that his dinner arrived when Turner was in his gallery with some great man, and the person (alleged by my informant to be his father) would whisper in the painter's ear, "that's ready". And then taking another turn round the gallery, he would again approach, and, in a somewhat louder whisper, say: "that's getting cold". At last, after another interval, he would say, louder still, "that's quite cold".

It is singular that Turner, who was so jealous of fame in his lifetime, should have been so careless to the goodness of his materials, sending, as a friend of his and my own remarked, for any colour he wanted to "the chap round the corner". The result of this indifference is that many, and to my certain knowledge one, of his best pictures is cracking all over. Though naturally fond of money, he allowed pictures to get mouldy in a cellar for which he might have got thousands; the alleged reason being that if the public did not buy them when they might, they should not when they pleased.

Aberdeen Journal, 24 November 1883

DID HENRY IRVING TREAD THE BOARDS WITH A WOODEN LEG?

[Henry Irving was the first actor to be awarded a knighthood. *Dracula* author Bram Stoker was his business manager.]

The American journals which more especially represent the stage confirm the impressions already given in private telegrams and letters as to Mr Irving's success in New York [starring as Matthias in *The Bells*]. *The Spirit of the Times* says: "New York has ratified the verdict of England, and the fame of Henry Irving is as secure in the New World as in the Old. His make-up is a study for our artistes; his performance ought to be attended by every actor and actress who desires to excel in the profession; his stage management should be a lesson to all our American managers."

Of the mannerisms *The Spirit* thus speaks: "During the first act the audience observed curiously Mr Irving's mannerisms, of which they had read and heard so much. He spoke in a strange hollow voice; he mumbled some of his words; he walked with an odd gait, as if one of his legs were wooden; but, every now and then there came a touch of nature, a flash of genius, which elicited instantaneous applause. The verdict at the end of the act was, 'He is very odd, but very fascinating.'

In the second act, whether the audience were becoming accustomed to Irving, or whether he was working himself free from his bizarre peculiarities, his grotesqueries were less noticeable, and the satisfaction of the audience more continuous. But in the third act all mannerisms were discarded, and the great actor was revealed without an imperfection. Never before has a dramatic dream been so perfectly represented upon our stage.

Cheltenham Looker-On, 15 December 1883

TIME FOR TENNYSON TO RAISE THE SARTORIAL BAR INSTEAD OF *CROSSING THE BAR*?

Now that Mr Gladstone has made the Poet Laureate a Peer, by the style and title of Lord Tennyson of D'Eyncourt, it is to be hoped that he will use his new influence with the Peer to induce him to conform in some respect to the customs and manners of the gentlemen who inhabit the "Gilded Chamber".

Probably, the titled Bard may eschew the shabby wide-awake hat and seedy Inverness cape in which he generally arrays his poetic person. Probably, too, he may include a "tail-coat" as when he recently accompanied Mr Gladstone in Sir Donald Currie's yacht to Copenhagen he was unable to accept an invitation to dine with the King because his travelling *impediments* was destitute of the evening dress which prosaic persons assume when invited to dinner!

Gloucester Citizen, 1 August 1899

DIVA'S SELF-IMAGE DIMINISHED BY OVER-DISTRIBUTION OF IMAGES

During her recent visit to London, [actress] Sarah Bernhardt scattered five-pound notes among scene-shifters and stage-carpenters in royal fashion. To one lucky fireman she presented, besides a large gratuity, a handsome photo of herself with a long dedication written across it in French, and only laughed when the sturdy recipient explained that he could not understand a word of it!

Apropos of Sarah's propensity for giving away signed photos of herself, the following story is told: Not very long ago she was driving through part of the Quartier Latin [Paris], when her eye caught sight of a large photo of herself displayed for sale in a tumble-down second-hand shop. She immediately alighted and inquired the price. The shop man, not recognising her, asked two francs.

"What, only two francs," cried the astonished actress, intent on reading the inscription, which was long and affectionate. "How can you sell it so cheap?" "Well, you see, Bernhardt gives away so many to artists and others that they are always trying to sell them for a few sous!" "I will never give away another," cried Sarah, and flounced out of the shop with her picture, leaving the shop man richer by 20f.

Hull Daily Mail, 25 June 1900

WIFE'S POOR PAY-OFF SINGING FOR HER SUPPER

Provoked By His Wife's Singing. At Beverley [Yorkshire] this morning a Joseph Wellburn was summoned for assaulting his wife. She said she went to fetch him from a public house, and on arriving home he gave her 19s only. She commenced singing, and he struck her, knocking her down. The Bench thought the defendant received provocation, and respited judgement for six months.

AMUSING MUSINGS
AND LIFE'S LITTLE FOIBLES

Ipswich Journal, 19 October 1771

DUKE'S TAXING PROBLEM OF PROMOTION

At the close of an election at Lewes, the late Duke of Newcastle was so delighted with the conduct of a casting voter, that he *almost fell upon his neck and kissed him.* "My dear friend I love you dearly! You're the greatest man in the world! I long to serve you! What can I do for you?" "May it please your Grace, an Excise man of this town is very old. I would beg leave to succeed him as soon as he shall die."

"Ay, that you shall with all my heart. I wish, for your sake, that he were dead and buried now! As soon as he is, set out to me my dear friend. Be it night or day, insist upon seeing me, sleeping or waking. If I am not at Claremont, come to Lincoln's Inn Fields, if I am not at Lincoln's Inn Fields come to court, if I am not at court never rest until you find me... Nay, I'll give orders for you to be admitted, though the King and I were talking secrets together in the cabinet."

The voter swallowed everything with ecstasy; and, scraping down to the very ground, retired to wait in faith for the death of the Excise man. The former took his leave of this wicked world in the following winter. As soon as ever the Duke's friend was apprised of it, he set off for London, and reached Lincoln's Inn Fields by about two o'clock in the morning.

The King of Spain had, about this time, been seized by a disorder, which some of the English had been induced to believe, from particular expresses, he could not possibly survive. Amongst these, the noble Duke was the most credulous, and probably the most anxious. On the very first moment of receiving his intelligence, he had dispatched couriers to Madrid, who were commanded to return with unusual haste, as soon as ever the death of his Catholic Majesty was announced. Ignorant of the hour in which they might arrive, and impatient of the fate of every hour, the Duke would not retire to his rest till he had given the strictest orders to his attendants, to send any person to his chamber who should desire admittance.

When the voter asked if he was at home, he was answered by the porter, "Yes; his grace has been in bed some time, but we are directed to awaken him as soon as ever you came." The happy visitor was scarcely conducted to the door, when he rushed into the room, and in the transport of his joy, cried out, "My Lord, he's dead."

"That's well, my dear friend, I am glad of it with all my soul. When did he die?"

"The morning before last."

"What, so lately? Why, my worthy good creature, you must have flown. The lightening itself could not travel half so fast as you. Tell me, you best of men, how shall I reward you?"

"All I wish for in this world is that your Grace would please to remember your kind promise, and appoint me to succeed him."

"You, you blockhead: you, King of Spain! What family pretensions can you have? Let's look at you."

By this time the astonished Duke threw back the curtains, and recollected the face of his electioneering friend; but it was seen with rage and disappointment. To have robbed him of his rest, might easily have been forgiven; but to have fed him with a groundless supposition that the King of Spain was dead, became a matter of resentment. He was at first dismissed with all the violence of anger and refusal.

At length, the victim of his passion became an object of his mirth; and, when he felt the ridicule that marked the incident, he raised the candidate for monarchy into a post which from the colour of the present times may seem at least as honourable – he made him an Excise man.

The British Chronicle, or, *Pugh's Hereford Journal* [sic],
15 September 1790

REWARD FOR SERVICES OVER AND ABOVE
THE CALL OF DUTY

There is in the vicinity of London a woman who has borne to her husband 22 children, all of whom grew up, and several of whom are living. She is full a stout woman, and is at present on the eve of lying in. Her husband, it must be remarked, is a Welshman. Query – Ought not such a couple to have a premium for their services to the State?

Yorkshire Gazette, 15 May 1819

BY HOOK OR BY LEGAL CROOK

Bishop Warburton, in giving his opinion of the Court of Chancery, observed: "As unfit as I am for heaven, I had rather hear the last trumpet, than a citation from the Court of Chancery. If ever you have seen Michael Angelo's *Last Judgment*, you have there, in the figure of the Devil, who is pulling and lugging at a poor sinner, the true representation of a Chancery lawyer, who has catched hold of your purse."

A PIG OF A NIGHT'S SLEEP

The late Rev. John Wesley, in a discourse he delivered in George Yard chapel, in Hull, asserted that six hours sleep was sufficient for man, seven hours for a woman, eight hours for a child, and nine hours for a pig.

Bath Chronicle and Weekly Gazette, 14 January 1830

THE DEVIL'S IN THE DETAIL

[Poet John] Milton and his descendants received for the entire copyright of *Paradise Lost* the sum of £28. R. Montgomery, the author of *Satan*, it is said, received from his publisher, for the copyright of that poem, nearly £1,000!

Blackburn Standard, 8 April 1835

THE DOHERTYS PUT ON A SHOW

At the Donegal Assizes James Doherty was indicted for an assault upon Dennis Doherty. It was a remarkable feature in this trial that the judge, the officiating clerk of the crown, the prosecutor, the prisoner, his counsel, his attorney, and the witnesses, pro and con, nine in number, were all Dohertys.

Woolmer's Exeter and Plymouth Gazette, 10 June 1837

HARD DRINKER IS A SHOO-IN FOR THE JOB

If you wish to have a shoe of durable materials, you should make the upper leather of the mouth of a hard drinker, for that never lets in water.

PURELY MEDICINAL ALCOHOL

A correspondent of the Boston Post states that certain gentlemen who keep temperance stores are licensed to keep alcohol as a medicine, and that they do a large business in this way, their customers generally being very much out of health.

Staffordshire Advertiser, 11 August 1838

QUEEN SUMMONED TO COURT FOR NON-PAYMENT OF RATES

Her Majesty the Queen Dowager [Adelaide] was summoned by the rate collectors of the parish of St. Martin to attend yesterday at the Westminster Petty Session, in the Broad Sanctuary, Westminster, to answer for the non-payment of £104, and some shillings, due to the parish of St. Martin as a quarter's poor rate for Her Majesty's residence, Marlborough House.

Her Majesty, it appears, was willing to pay the rate demanded as a donation, but she objected to pay it as a rate. This, the parish refused to accede to, and the present proceedings were instituted.

On the opening of the court, Mr. Sergeant Merewether, Her Majesty's Solicitor-General, was in attendance; but in consequence of some arrangement which was entered into between the Learned Sergeant on the part of Her Majesty, and the representatives of the parish (the precise nature of which did not transpire) the further consideration of the case was, by consent, adjourned to Tuesday next, the 14th August. [It was ultimately agreed to accept the money as a donation.]

Wiltshire Independent, 16 August 1838

ATTORNEY'S THUMBS-UP TO OMNIBUS LADIES' KNEES-UP

Omnibus Practices. In the course of an investigation on Tuesday at the Mansion House, where a young man was suspected of having intended to rob a lady in an omnibus, from having been seen moving his hand towards her pocket, under cover of his mackintosh, the following dialogue took place between the prisoner's attorney and a gentleman who attended as a witness for the prosecution:

—Attorney: Pray did you never observe a gentleman in an

omnibus put his hand upon a lady's knee? —Witness: Yes.

—Attorney: Don't you know that such a thing is frequently done, and with the endeavour to escape the observation of others?

—Witness: I believe that such is the case.

The attorney added, that if persons were to be suspected of dishonesty because they put their hand upon ladies' knees in an omnibus, many a gentleman would suffer unjustly.

Windsor and Eton Express, 2 March 1839

THE GOOD BOOK REPELS EVIL FORCES OF HELL-FIRE FLAMES

An Extraordinary Fact. Connected with the recent conflagration at Fermoy, Ireland, in which Mrs. Wall and her entire household property perished, there is a circumstance which can scarcely be accounted for on mere natural principles.

It is this: that a Bible, which had been placed on a shelf among several other books, escaped the fire, and had been found among the ruins, with no other injury save that of being much soiled on the outside. Not a vestige of any of the books among which it had been placed could be found, and so destructive was the fire that not a single portion of the remains of Mrs. Wall were found, nor any other which fire could take effect.

Leamington Spa Courier, 4 May 1839

JAMES BOND WOULD HAVE MADE A SONG AND DANCE OVER THESE BOOTS

Among the curious inventions exhibited in the French capital during the year was a pair of defensive boots, having in each of the legs a pistol, immediately under the sole a little case for bank-notes, and in each end a dagger, arms both sufficiently portable and defensive; and a musical instrument, which serves either for a violin or a pitcher(!), being made of baked clay in a very curious manner.

Liverpool Mercury, 26 August 1842

NOVEL APPROACH TO JUDGING SUITABILITY OF YOUNG LADIES

No doubt about it. An American paper says that young ladies who are accustomed to reading newspapers are always observed to possess winning ways, most amiable dispositions and invariably make good wives; while on the other hand those who read nothing, or what is far worse – *novels*, are generally unfit for either society or domestic cares, and their company but little sought for by either sex, further than the rules of common civility actually requires.

A TAXING OCCUPATION FOR A JOBSWORTH

"There is nothing new under the sun." So thought Solomon; but Sir Robert Peel has brought a new trade into existence – that of filling up income-tax papers – a trade now regularly advertised in several parts of the country.

REPORT OF THE EARLIEST TWEET?

The following truly Spartan communication was received the other day by a Liverpool merchant from another merchant and correspondent: "Sir, I shall be over next week. Yours respectfully,___"

BLEAK BOARDING-HOUSE BILL

A Bait. A London boarding-house keeper is advertising that she has taken the furnished residence of Mr. Charles Dickens, and intends to lodge friends in it. Only think – to sleep in Charles Dickens' bed at five shillings a night!

SACRE BLEU! WAR-HORSE PLAY AT THE *GREAT EXHIBITION*

Amongst the visitors to the *Great Exhibition* last Wednesday week was the Duke of Wellington, accompanied by his daughter-in-law, the Marchioness of Douro. After walking down the transept, the noble and gallant Duke turned into the French department, and paused to observe one of the exhibitors removing from an oaken case various articles of silver and gold plate. Among the *morceaux* [pieces] uncovered as the Duke walked up were a pair of silver equestrian statuettes, representing the Duke himself, and his once formidable rival, Napoleon. The great Captain smiled at the incident, and to an inquiring look of the French artist, nodded his assent.

The news instantly spread that the Duke of Wellington was within the "French territory", and for a very few moments – probably for the first time in his life – the noble and gallant Duke was surprised and surrounded by a body of Frenchmen. Happily, in the present instance, the national character for politeness prevailed over every other feeling. The hats and caps of the bearded strangers were instinctively raised to Great Britain's "hero," and the noble Duke having returned a military salute, passed on to the next department.

Leicester Chronicle, 11 November 1854

A GUARDED RESPONSE TO A PROBING QUESTION

A country youth, who had returned from the city, was asked by his anxious father if he had been guarded in his conduct while there? "Oh, yes," was the reply, "I was guarded by two policemen part of the time."

Norfolk Chronicle, 23 August 1856

A DEADLY YET SPIRITED MARRIAGE

A young man residing in Bordentown [New Jersey, USA], who was under an engagement of marriage with a young lady, died on Friday last. Both the gentleman and lady, as well as their families, were firm believers in the doctrines of the spiritualists, and notwithstanding the death of the former, it was determined that the marriage should take place between the disembodied spirit of the man, and the living, breathing body of his affianced bride. Accordingly, on Sunday, the marriage ceremony was performed between the clay cold corpse and the warm, blooming bride. It is understood that this was in compliance with the directions of the spirit bridegroom. *Trenton Gazette* (U. S.) August 5.

The Westmorland Gazette, 18 September 1858

SIMPLE PARENTING ADVICE

Taxidermy for parents: If you want to preserve your children, do not stuff them.

Worcestershire Chronicle, 30 November 1859

IMPERIAL DRESS CODE ALL SEWN UP

Dresses at Compiegne, from the Paris Correspondent of the *Literary Gazette*. Four toilettes [formal sets of clothes] a day are about the general requirements of Imperial etiquette, though there are days when only three are necessary; the invitations are for eight days, and no lady is expected ever to be seen twice wearing the same gown. Count this up, an average of 32 toilettes to be carried down to the Court. Suppose a female invitee not to be alone, but to have a daughter (or two daughters) with her – you come at once to 90 or 96 dresses!

Hereford Times, 28 February 1863

JOLLY GOOD FUN BY ROYAL COMMAND – NO SPOILSPORTS ALLOWED

Sports of the Last Century. Here are the amusements which entertained George III and his daughters. A handbill invites "all persons of jovial, friendly, and loyal dispositions" to be present at the under-mentioned country sports: "A barrel of beer be rolled down hill – prize to whoever stops it. A pound of tobacco, to be grinned for. A handsome hat for the boy most expert at catching a roll dipped in treacle." *The Spectator.*

Cambridge Chronicle and Journal, 6 April 1867 and
Dunfermline Saturday Press, 10 August 1867

EERIE DESCRIPTION OF FALSE EAR FASHION

Important to Donkeys. False ears of flesh colour india-rubber have been invented for the use of ladies with large ears. They are used in front of the real ears, which are drawn back and concealed under the hair.

CAUTION BACHELORS

A contemporary says that small neat gutta-percha [natural latex] ears are now generally worn by ladies whose own ears are coarse and excessive, the natural ears being easily concealed under the heavy masses of false hair now so fashionable. It will soon be necessary – indeed it is now necessary – that a man taking a woman to wife should obtain a surgical certificate as to the genuineness of her charms. What must be the feelings of the bridegroom who discovers that he mated with a partner who wears a false eye, false hair, false teeth, and false bozoms, and whose complexion has been made beautiful forever by the Arabian enamel and Circassian cosmetics of Rachael and Co.?

Shields Daily Gazette, 7 June 1867

WINNER OF THE MOST IMPORTANT SOCIAL INVENTION BY A WHISKER

I was much struck the other day by a novel and important invention which I saw in a shop window. This was nothing more nor less than a set of tea-things specially adapted for the use of gentlemen who cultivate moustaches, the cups of which have a band running across them of sufficient width to prevent the moustache from having a warm bath when its owner sips his tea and yet allowing free play to the lips, on one side of it, and the nose on the other.

An invention pre-supposes a want. The love of tea taking so much the place of the love of wine that moustached heroes have been crying out for more comfort in the drinking of it? For some great genius of inventive power who will come forward and show them how to protect their well-beloved ornaments – how to keep them intact during the vicissitudes of a tea-fight, free from the forlorn and drowned appearance that they now present, after having gone through one of these mildest of actions... to such men a moustache-cup will offer a silent but unmistakeable hint, and society generally will feel the benefit of this advent of porcelain reformers.

Aberdeen Evening Express, 20 January 1879

CLOTHING THE NAKED

No profession is as squeamish as the legal. Let a solicitor come across any bare facts, and he is well nigh sure to wrap them up in a law suit as soon as he can.

DAVID GARRICK STANDS UP TO HIS CRITICS

Said a lady to the famous actor Garrick [1717–1779]: "I wish you were taller." "Madam," replied the wit, "how happy I should be to stand higher in your estimation!"

Illustrated Police News, 22 April 1882

MON DIEU! THOUSANDS OF FROGS CROAK-IT TO END UP AS AN AMERICAN DELICACY

A new company has been started at Maine [USA] to supply eastern cities with canned frogs' legs. Factories are being built for that purpose.

Evening Telegraph, 7 September 1891

STRAPPING LAWN-TENNIS LADIES HAVING A BALL WITH THE PRINCE OF WALES

A pleasant little sketch of the Prince of Wales at Homburg is given in the lively description of that resort in Saturday's *Speaker*. Frank and outspoken in talk, with a ringing laugh, and a roll in his walk like the great King Harry, whom he more than ever resembles, he seemed, says the writer, to give the lie at every instant to the rumours of his embarrassments and malaise.

For 14 hours a day, for 20 days last past, he has lived in the sight of hundreds of his future subjects, offending no-one, making no favourites, equally genial and at home with the diverse crowd whom could recognise as his acquaintance, old or new. He has desired no extraneous means of amusement to be provided for him, living on the same victuals and sharing the same rather hum-drum amusements as the crowd – seemingly best pleased when patting his faithful Spitz dog, now old, lame, and partly blind, or talking to a little child, or perhaps promenading with a strapping "lawn-tennis" girl of the English middle-class.

Leeds Times, 22 August 1896

IF ONLY IT HAD BEEN A DUCK HOUSE INSTEAD OF A HAT

[Li Hung Chang, later written as Li Hongzhang (15 February 1823–7 November 1901), was a politician, General, and diplomat of the late Qing Empire. He was made a Knight Grand Cross of the Royal Victorian Order by Queen Victoria during his visit to Britain in 1896.]

As Li Hung Chang visited the House of Commons while the "foreign devils" were discussing the Scotch [sic] Rating Bill, he ought, says *Sketch*, to be made acquainted with a moving incident of the debate. The English members took very little interest in the debate, which related to matters quite beyond their comprehension; but one Englishman, moved by a sense of duty, tried very hard to understand what was going on.

Presently he went to sleep, and a Scotch member sitting next to him rose to make a speech. Still the Englishman slept, till suddenly the Scotch member sat down on his hat. Then the English member awoke, and, with whispered maledictions, devoted everything Scotch to the infernal gods.

By the way, it is not etiquette, I understand, for a member who sits down on another member's hat to buy the sufferer a new one. The destruction of a hat is supposed to be one of the natural vicissitudes of public life.

Yorkshire Evening Post, 24 March 1899

CALLING TIME – LANDLORDS PUT SPOKE IN CYCLISTS' WHEELS

In Yorkshire, as in the South of England, the landlord has come to loggerheads with the cyclists. Not long ago the proprietor of a hotel was arraigned before his betters, charged with the offence of refusing to supply cyclists with reasonable refreshments.

In Bradford and Leeds the same trouble has arisen, which goes far to prove that the grievance of which cyclists complain, far from being imaginary, is, on the contrary, a very general one. Even the humble pedestrian is interested in the question, for when he takes his walks abroad into the country he is not always inclined to drink ale and be content with the inevitable onion and cheese.

To the credit of the landlords of Yorkshire, it must be said that they cater very well for their customers, and that they compare very favourably with their brethren. But there are landlords and landlords. Some of those can upon occasion be as ostentatiously disobliging as only the puffed-up aristocrats of Bungdom know how.

The teetotal cyclist, somehow, seems to be his pet aversion. It is all very well for Boniface to plead that owing to his numerous candidates for the beer mug he is too busy to make tea for cyclists. It is as much his duty by virtue of his licence to refresh the cyclist as to slake the thirst of the lounger. There is a mistaken idea on the part of both pedestrians and cyclists that they can command a landlord to minister their wants.

Some indignant wayfarers have even sent for the police to

move a stubborn host, only to learn that the policeman is powerless in the matter. It is as absurd for a cyclist to suppose that he can compel a landlord to serve him as to imagine that he can force a stranger to entertain him hospitably. The cyclist's best remedy, however, when he has a grievance, lies with the licensing magistrates.

Sunderland Daily Echo and Shipping Gazette, 11 August 1903

WAS THIS LETTER SENT BY SEA-MAIL WRITTEN IN OCTOPUS INK?

The Captain of the steamer *Benalder*, of Leith, having thrown overboard a bundle of 20 old letters in the Mediterranean on his voyage to China, they have again come to light in the following manner: Some fishermen, noticing a corpulent fish amongst their catch, opened it, and found a bundle of letters. They took them to the Mayor of Aguilas, a Spanish fishing town, who delivered them to the British Consul. He, upon examination, found only one letter decipherable, and has just forwarded it to the writer, Capt. Potter, the superintendent in London, as he thought the peculiar circumstances of its recovery might interest him.

Bath Chronicle and Weekly Gazette, 27 December 1913

WHEELS OF JUSTICE TURN IN MYSTERIOUS WAYS

Sympathetic Bench in fast driving charge. "We look upon the act of taking a clergyman to catch a train very much in the same light as that of a doctor being taken to see a patient. The driver was not driving fast for the sake of it and the Bench agree to the withdrawal of the summons on payment of two guineas as costs." These were the remarks by the Manchester County Stipendiary on Tuesday in a case where Samuel Williamson, a chauffeur, of Blanche Cottages, Lynn, and in the employ of Mr. Thomas Wilson, of Lynn, was summoned for driving a motor car at a speed dangerous to the public along Chester Road, Stretford, December 6th.

Evening Telegraph, 12 November 1926

TIME TO GIVE THIS QUACKERS DIAGNOSIS A REST

A doctor has been recommending floor scrubbing as a rest cure. He has discovered that charwomen rather enjoy scrubbing floors on all fours, and that the same is true of elementary schoolgirls undergoing cookery training. They actually spill water as an excuse for going down on their hands and knees to wipe it up. The idea is that going down on all fours is a reminiscence of the time when we were quadrupeds, and therefore a reversion to a primitive instinct. But I think I could explain it better than that. The compelling idea in the scrubbing is not the all fours position but the joy of dabbling in water. All children like that. Clearly it is a reminiscence of the time, not when we were quadrupeds, but when we were fish.

The Yorkshire Post and Leeds Intelligencer, 21 April 1930

CLUB FOR HENPECKED HUSBANDS RANKS TOP OF THE PECKING ORDER

Strange Clubs. Easter Monday is the date of the annual outing of the *Henpecked Husbands' Club*, which has its headquarters at Sowerby Bridge. This famous Yorkshire club, whose full title is *Ancient and Honourable and International Order of Henpecked Husbands*, is undoubtedly the most noted of all Britain's queer societies.

It is said that it never lacks candidates for membership, although they must prove they have been henpecked for at least two years, and must answer to what household tasks, such as washing-up and bed-making, they have been humiliated. Its secrets are jealously guarded, and the annual picnic is held at some lonely moorland spot, which all members are forbidden to divulge.

Once upon a time, the North could boast of another curious body, which had its headquarters at Manchester and was known as the *Anti-Suicide Club*, every member which had at some time or other attempted to commit suicide, and had presumably resolved never to try again.

The Thirteen Club, who meet on April 13 and do all they can to bring ill luck on themselves in defiance of superstition, are well-known. Then there is *The Hearty Eaters' Club*, whose members partake of dinner of a hundred courses, *The Fat Men's Club*... and *The Quiet Club*, of which [conductor] Sir Henry Wood was an original member, together with [violinist and composer Fritz] Kreisler and [composer] Sir E. Elgar.

ALL IN A DAY'S WORK

LUDICROUS PUNISHMENT for CRUELTY to A DONKEY

Police Gazette, 17 February 1775

GOING THE EXTRA MILE TO DELIVER GOOD SERVICE

Eleven fenmen [residents of the marshy lowland region known as the Fens of England] from the Isle of Ely, being employed by Sir John Griffin, in training a part of his park at Audley End, went one evening to the Inn called The Hoops, to drink. After getting a little spirited, they told the maid, they would give sixpence each to fetch them as much beer they could drink, in half-pints out of the cellar; if they tired her, she was to pay for the liquor; if she tired them, they were to pay for the whole. The girl accepted the bet, although she had been washing all the day, and drew them 517 single half-pints [0.28 litres], before they gave out, which were all drank by the said men. The distance from the room where they sat, to the tap, was measured, from which it appears she walked near 12 miles in fetching it; and the quantity of liquor drank by each man was about three gallons [13.6 litres] in three hours. The above is the real fact.

Hereford Journal, 4 January 1781

CROSS-DRESSING THIEF GETS A DRESSING DOWN

Yesterday a young woman in a man's dress was committed to the New Jail, Southwark, for robbing some persons the night before, at a public house in Kennington Place. She proves to be Anne Wilson, who in the same habit has committed many highway robberies on the several roads round this metropolis; and is ordered by the Justice to retain her dress until trial.

Newcastle Courant, 9 August 1806

ROYAL BED-FELLOW IN CRIME WITH A MAGNIFICENT CHINESE TAKE-AWAY

The furniture of a superb state bed was lately worked in China and intended as a present to the Spanish Prince of Peace. The ship in which it was sent, having been captured by a British vessel, this magnificent piece of furniture was purchased by Mr Goldsmid, who has since presented it to the Prince of Wales [George IV]. The ground work is of the most beautiful yellow satin. The counterpane represents the Empress of China seated in state, giving audience to a number of figures, who are most exquisitely delineated in the costume of the country. Mr Goldsmid had been offered 500 pounds for his bargain. The Prince, extremely delighted with so appropriate a present, has ordered it to be placed in the state bed-chamber, in his Chinese pavilion, at Brighton.

Taunton Courier and Western Advertiser, 24 May 1820

A DEAD CERTAINTY FOR REVULSION

The Campo Santo, the great *Golgotha* [place of burial] of Naples. It is situated on rising ground behind the town, about a mile and half from the gate. Within its walls are 365 caverns; one is open every day for the reception of the dead, the great mass whom, as soon the rites of religion have been performed, are brought here for sepulchre.

There were 15 cast in, while we were there; men, women, and children, without a rag to cover them, literally fulfilling the words of the Scripture: "As he came forth out of his mother's womb, naked shall he return, to go as he came." I looked down into this frightful charnel house – it was a shocking sight – a mass of blood and garbage, for many of the bodies had been opened at the hospitals. Cockroaches and other reptiles were crawling about in all their glory.

We made the sexton of this dreary abode who, by the way, had been employed in this daily work for 11 years, open the stone of the next day's grave, which had been sealed up for a year. The flesh was entirely gone, for in such a fermenting mass, the work of corruption must go on swimmingly; quick lime is added to hasten the process and nothing seemed to remain, but a dry heap of bones and skulls. What must be the feelings of those, who can suffer the remains of a friend, a sister, a mother, or a wife, to be thus disposed of?

Belfast News-Letter, 1 January 1828

NO SCALING-BACK TEMPTATION

A female servant, considerably advanced beyond the equinox of life, availed herself of the supposed liberty of conscience which Christmas brings with it for the free indulgence both of the eating and drinking propensities. From Tuesday till Saturday, one round of intoxication regularly succeeded another, till the festive orgies became no longer tolerable, and a dismissal was the consequence.

Early on Saturday morning she contrived to re-enter her master's house. On a chimney-piece of a little parlour was a large decanter, which had been hermetically sealed, containing some Demerara snakes, in a state of preservation. Some time before it had been injured, and the original fluid having escaped, it had lately been replaced with common spirits as a substitute.

The temptation was irresistible; she seized the decanter and actually drank the whisky off the snakes! A tremendous scene followed but fortunately the poison had been either absorbed by the original fluid, or animal poisons when taken into the stomach are innoxious.

The Kendal Mercury and Westmorland Advertiser, 17 March 1838

HANDY SOLUTION NEEDED TO OVERCOME THIS CHEEKY FORM OF SLOBBERING HOMAGE!

There is a report that the Coronation is to take place in August. The difference in the forms and ceremonies that will be the consequence of the Sovereign being female are already beginning to be discussed, and will, no doubt, soon find employment for the officials of the Herald's College.

There is no doubt that these personages would render the Queen an essential, or at any rate, an acceptable service, if they could by any possibility find a precedent for dispensing with, or at least altering, the form of the homage of the Peers. As it is, Her Majesty will have received the kisses of 600 old gentlemen on this occasion.

The homage is performed thus: the bishops and archbishops first, kneeling before the Sovereign, the Archbishop Canterbury saying aloud, and the rest of the bishops following him, "I, William, Archbishop of Canterbury (and so the rest of the bishops) will be faithful and true, and faith and truth will bear unto you our Sovereign Lord (Lady) and your heirs, Kings of the United Kingdom, Great Britain and Ireland. And I will do, and truly acknowledge the service of the lands which I claim to hold of you, as in right of the Church, so help me God.

The Archbishop and bishops then get up, and kiss the Sovereign's left cheek. Then the temporal Peers (each class separately) follow. After the oath has been pronounced the Peers rise but still remain unbonneted, and each Peer, according to his rank and precedence, singly ascends the throne, and touches with his hand the crown on the Sovereign's head, and kisses her cheek.

Now, as it is not likely that many Peers would be absent on so interesting an occasion as the coronation of our young Queen, Her Majesty will have to undergo a rather severe infliction in the *chaste solute* [chaste solution] by the Lords spiritual and temporal.

Wiltshire Independent, 16 August 1838

VATICAN SHEDS LIGHT ON GOD'S WORK

Such is the danger and frequent loss of life in effecting the splendid illuminations of the dome of St. Peter's [Basilica] during the Holy Week, that the workmen invariably receive absolution previous to entering upon their employment.

Liverpool Mercury, 26 August 1842

MAGISTRATE SWALLOWS IMPROBABLE DEFENCE

Singular cure for the bowel complaint. John Wills, the driver of car [carriage] 141, appeared before the magistrates on Friday, to answer a complaint which had been lodged against him for being so much intoxicated as to be unable to follow his usual calling. It appeared that he had been wanted to convey a gentleman from Castle Street to Clayton Square, and that he was found stretched upon the inside of his car, with his legs extending out at the doorway and over the steps.

The fellow set up a singular form of defence. He said that he had been seriously attacked with a bowel complaint, and that, after having obtained a dose of castor oil from Mr. Butler, druggist, of Castle Street, with the view of therewith effecting a cure, he met an old friend, a gentleman who professed to have great skill in the pharmaceutical department, and who told him that a glass of water containing a hot cinder was a far more effectual cure than all the castor oil in Butler's shop.

Wills, simple soul!, stated that he believed the tale, and that, after having swallowed the water, (he omitted to say whether he swallowed the cinder also), it had the extraordinary effect of making his head heavier than his heels, and producing all the appearance of intoxication. He, moreover, called the cinder doctor, who deposed to his having given the prescription, and who still stoutly defended the efficacy of his cure. Mr Rushton gave Wills the benefit of the doubt which the case implied, and ordered him to be discharged.

Bath Chronicle, 24 April 1851

PAYMENT COCK-UP

Money-taking Extraordinary. Mr. Bochsa having, with Madame Anna Bishop, given a concert in one of the towns of the interior of Mexico, was rather startled, when the gallery money-taker came to him to pay over the takings of the evening, to find that those takings consisted of numerous pieces of yellow soap, lots of cigars, two live fighting cocks, and sundry other articles of "small money" current in the interior. Mr. Bochsa proceeded to pay the money-taker's salary, which amounted to four pieces of soap and a packet of cigars. The game cocks proved the most readily convertible portion of this curious currency, and were at once spitted and put down to the fire.

Stamford Mercury, 6 August 1852

GHASTLY AND GHOSTLY RETRIBUTION FROM BEYOND THE GRAVE

Very recently the deputy-coroner held an inquest on the body of Geo. Roe, of Nettleham, a steady money-saving man, who worked the farm of Ald. Rudgard. *Coup de soleil* [sunburn] was the verdict. After the burial of the deceased, his widow removed to Scothern, and a few days since died there.

A statement is now afloat that the husband had saved 30L. [pounds] which the wife had discovered and spent; that a disturbance occurred, and she threatened to do for him; that she took him some coffee into the field, and shortly after he vomited and was purged violently (these were not stated to the deputy-coroner), and became insensible; that after his death she procured 10L. from a funeral club; that afterwards, she complained that the deceased haunted her and she removed, but he still haunted her; that she then poisoned herself, after attempting to commit suicide by hanging; and that upon her death-bed she confessed to having poisoned her husband, and that both arsenic and laudanum were found in the house.

Leeds Intelligencer, 23 July 1853

HOW TO PAPER OVER THE CRACKS OF A HOUSING CRISIS IN AN ENVIRONMENTALLY-FRIENDLY WAY

Messrs. Bielefeld have commenced the manufacture of papier-mâché houses. The framework, the flooring, and the doors are of wood, but the rest is constructed of paper. A number of cottages, stores, and villas have been erected at Messrs. Bielefeld's works at Staines; and a gentleman has purchased them as an investment for Australia, whither he is going. These buildings can readily be taken down, and re-erected in a few hours. They have hollow walls, so that damp is excluded; and tropical insects will not attack the paper, for the poisonous ingredients it contains.

Carlisle Journal, 4 January 1856

HOLY TAP-WATER! FOR GOD'S SAKE, GIVE US THIS DAY OUR DAILY DRINK! DRINK! MORE DRINK!

Sir J. Dodson gave judgment in the Arches Court, in the case of the Rev. R. West, rector of Pett, Sussex. He was charged with drunkenness, using profane language, and other offences.

In June, 1854 he went from Rye to Folkestone in his private yacht, and put up at the Hotel de Paris. There he got drunk after dinner and went to the fair, dressed as a sailor, and gave himself out to be a Captain in the navy. In September he went to

Boulogne, where, during his three days' stay, he was constantly in liquor. In October he dined with about 40 men in a public house at Rye harbour, whence he returned home intoxicated in a carriage, some of his drunken companions being with him, inside and outside.

In December, he was "vinous" at the rectory house, and in the course of the evening, when some musicians came to the house, he directed the servants to dance and attempted to do so himself, putting his arms round the waists of his female servants; in September last he thrashed a waggoner who would not allow his carriage to pass.

In April, being intoxicated, he visited one of his female parishioners who was in a dying state; on leaving her bedroom he put his arm round her daughter's neck and attempted to kiss her, using at the same time some very improper language. The latter charge was not satisfactorily proved. He was suspended for two years, and condemned with costs.

Norfolk Chronicle, 23 August 1856

SO WHOSE TURN WAS IT TO DO THE WASHING UP?

As banquets for our brave soldiers are now in vogue, and it is proposed to give a grand dinner to the Guards on their return to the metropolis, the readers of *Notes and Queries* may be glad to learn that the greatest dinner ever known in England was that given by Lord Romney to the Kent volunteers on August 1, 1709, when George III reviewed them near Maidstone.

The tables, amounting to 91 in number, were seven miles and a half long, and the boards for the tables cost £1,500. The entertainment, to which 6,500 persons sat down, consisted of 60 lambs in quarters, 200 dishes of roast beef, 700 fowls (three in a dish), 220 meat pies, 300 hams, 300 tongues, 220 fruit pies, 220 dishes of boiled beef, 220 joints of roast veal. Seven pipes [lengthy barrels of variable size holding on average 550 litres or around 700 bottles] of port were bottled-off and 16 butts of ale, and as much small beer was also placed in large vessels, to supply the company.

Whitstable Times and Herne Bay Herald, Saturday 1 July 1871

PICKLED STRAWBERRY-PICKERS

London has again been visited, since the thunderstorms of last week, with intensely cold weather. On Monday morning there was a sharp frost. So cold is it in the suburbs on the banks of the Thames that the strawberry-pickers, who do their work at 3am in the morning, having gin served out to keep their fingers from being benumbed.

Bradford Daily Telegraph, 9 January 1875

THE ROAD TO WIGAN FEAR

Wigan has narrowly escaped a terrible disaster. On Saturday a drunken carter was observed driving throughout the town a horse drawing a cart laden with about a ton [1016 kgs] of gunpowder, the barrels containing which were only partially covered by a tarpaulin. The police took possession of the vehicle, and locked up the driver, who was described as having been very drunk.

The danger of an explosion was enhanced by the fact that the road was very slippery, and that the carter, who was seated on the cart, had in his possession a number of *Lucifer* matches. The magistrate fined the man 20s. for being drunk, and on Thursday his employer appeared at the police court to answer a charge of conveying the powder in question through the streets without its being properly covered. The magistrate ordered the forfeiture of the powder, which was valued at £40.

Illustrated Police News, 22 January 1876

MADE TO FEEL A RIGHT ASS

An extraordinary scene took place on Saturday last at a small village within three miles of Middleton. A half-witted fellow named James Driscott had cruelly ill-used his donkey. He was told by several of the villagers that he would be brought up before the magistrates and severely punished; but his informants said that if he consented to do penance for his inhuman conduct, no information should be laid against him. Driscott gladly agreed to the proposed terms. The donkey was placed in the cart, and its owner, with the collar round his neck, was constrained to drag his four-footed servant through the village. The scene is described by a local reporter as being the most laughter-moving one he had ever witnessed.

Aberdeen Journal, 24 November 1883

WOULD FATHER CADFAEL HAVE
SOLVED THIS CRIME?

A peasant has been shot in the convent of Casamari, near Veroli [Italy], by a monk, under the following circumstances: The monks of that convent having perceived that the grain in the granary was fast disappearing, one of the monks of the name of Fra [Brother] Michele was posted one night in a corner of the granary, armed with a loaded musket. Late at night a peasant approached the convent wall with a ladder. No sooner had the unfortunate man entered the granary than he fell dead, shot by the monk.

Sheffield Evening Telegraph, 23 December 1887

D'OYLY CARTE BLANCHE TO DO
AS SOME DAY IT MAY HAPPEN

An English Pooh-Bah. *Truth* describes the duties of an English official at Labuan, a possession of this country in North Borneo, who seems to have as many functions as Pooh-Bah of *The Mikado*. There are only two English officials, Governor Leys and Lieutenant Hamilton. The latter gentleman combines in himself the offices of colonial secretary, postmaster, treasurer, magistrate, inspector of police, inspector of the prison, chief commissioner of woods, colonial engineer, and master attendant. In these various capacities he corresponds from himself to himself in the most stately official style, and carefully copies and registers his numerous despatches.

Aberdeen Journal, 25 August 1890

HOLY SPECTACLE! FIVE HUNDRED
CLERYGMEN AT THE THEATRE

It was a curious audience (remarks a London correspondent) which assembled at Mr Willard's invitation in the Shaftesbury Theatre on Thursday. With the exception of a little knot of press men, almost the whole of the males present were clergymen of all denominations.

Some of the timid refused the invitation on the score of holidays, but that the clergy of the present day do not hold respectably conducted theatres in the horror which London persons used to affect was abundantly shown by the presence of upwards of 500 wearers of 'the cloth'.

The play, of course, was *Judah*, and it would be interesting if Mr Willard were eventually to publish, though of course without mentioning the names of their authors, the opinions which will doubtless be privately or by letter conveyed to him of an audience which, so far as the performance of stage plays is concerned, is probably unique in the history of theatres.

Evening Telegraph, 7 September 1891

RAILROADED BY DEATH INTO PAYING LESS WAGES?

The North British Railway Company are, says the *N.B. Mail*, saving money by the death of their old manager, Mr Walker, who fought and crushed the greatest railway strike of modern times. He got £3,000 a year. His successor, Mr Connacher, is to get only £1,800. Still, this is a large rise for him, because as manager of the Cambrian Railways his salary was only £500 a year.

Yorkshire Evening Post, 24 March 1899

10 – 1 KIPLING'LL MAKE IT

Throughout her recent heavy trials Mrs. Kipling [wife of Rudyard] proved herself a devoted wife and tender, patient mother. Night after night she watched by the bedside of her famous husband, whose life hung by a thread [due to pneumonia]. Then her little daughters were down, and Mrs. Kipling, notwithstanding the commands of the doctors, insisted upon helping to nurse them too. One evening – it was the evening when we had news that Kipling's crisis was past – a writer in the "West End" was reading his paper in the hansom that conveyed him home. As he stepped out he handed the paper to the cabman. "Kipling's all right," he said. The cabman took the paper, and leaned down with a puzzled look on his face. "Don't seem to know the name o' the 'awse," [horse] he said.

ANIMAL ANTICS
AND CREATURE CONFUSION

The Birmingham Gazette or the General Correspondent [sic],
16 November 1741

MAYHEM AS MAD COW STORMS PUB ... MAYBE THIRSTING FOR A GLASS OF BULL'S BLOOD?

As a mad cow was driving [being driven] from Smithfield, she ran up the yard of the King's Arms Inn at Holborn bridge, and having drove all the people into close quarters, she went upstairs into the first gallery; but not liking any room there, broke several windows, then went up the second gallery. After visiting the rooms there she jumped over the rails upon the shed put up for the convenience of loading wagons, and with her weight broke through the tiling and fell to the ground, and by the fall broke her back which prevented further mischief.

Oxford Journal , 19 October 1771

GOADING A GOAT

Sunday morning last, a large He-Goat, finding the street door of a gentleman's house at Highgate open, walked into the parlour, where there was a large looking-glass, and thinking he saw one of his Welsh Brethren, ran his horns with such force against the glass, that he broke it into several pieces.

Staffordshire Advertiser, 3 August 1799

LIONS THAT WERE REALLY PUSSY CATS

The following incident has attracted much notice at Paris: – Citizen Felix two years ago brought two lions, male and female, to the National Menagerie. About the beginning of June, Felix fell ill, and could no longer attend the lions; another was forced to do his duty.

The lion, sad and solitary, remained from that moment

constantly seated at the end of his cage, and refused to receive anything from the stranger. His presence even was hateful to him, and he menaced him by bellowing. The company even of the female seemed to displease; he paid no attention to her. The uneasiness of the animal afforded a belief that he was really ill, but no one dared approach him.

At length Felix got well, and meaning to surprise the lion he crawled softly to the cage, and showed only his face against the bars; the lion in a moment made a bound, leaped against the bars, patted him with his paws, licked his hands and face, and trembled with pleasure. The female ran to him also; the lion drove her back, seemed angry, fearful that she should snatch any favours from Felix: a quarrel seemed about to take place between them, but Felix entered the cage to pacify them. He caressed them by turns.

Felix is now seen frequently in the midst of this formidable couple, whose power he has fettered; he holds a kind of conversation with them. Does he wish that they should separate and retire each to their cages? He has only to speak a word. Does he wish that they should lie down and show strangers their paws armed with terrible claws, and their throats full of tremendous teeth?

At the least sign from him they lie on their backs, hold up their paws one after another, open their throats, and as recompense, obtain the favour of licking his hand. These two animals, of a strong breed, are five years and a half old; they were both of the same mother and have always lived together.

Westmorland Gazette, 27 June 1818

DID GROGGY SAILORS SEE SEA SERPENT AFTER TOO MUCH GROG?

Capt. Woodward, and the mate and seamen of the schooner *Adamant*, which arrived at Hingham on Sunday last from Penobscot, saw, in the afternoon of the day previous, about 12 leagues [41.5

miles] east of Cape Ann [north of Boston], a sea serpent, apparently upwards of 100 feet [30.48 metres] long, which frequently raised its head a considerable height from the water. It was very near the vessel for about five hours; a full view was had of it, and it appeared to be about as large round as a barrel, but no protuberances were noticed. It was once fired at and appeared irritated by the explosion. *Boston Palladium.*

The Manchester Courier and Lancashire General Advertiser,
26 March 1825

DOG FEELS RUFF-RUFF DUE TO
FROG IN ITS THROAT

We have been informed from a very creditable source that a dog, the property of a person residing at William Street, Moricetown, Devonport, on Monday last, vomited 13 living toads, 11 of which were small and two nearly full grown.

Northampton Mercury, 28 April 1832

THE APPRENTICE BOOT-LEGGER ALAN SUGAR
WOULD BE PROUD OF

An officer in the 44th regiment, who had occasion when in Paris to pass one of the bridges across the Seine, had his boots, which were previously well polished, dirtied by a poodle dog rubbing against them. He, in consequence, went to a man who was stationed on the bridge, and had them cleaned.

The same circumstance having occurred more than once, his curiosity was excited, and he watched the dog. He saw him roll himself in the mud of the river and then watch for a person with well-polished boots against which he contrived to rub himself against.

Finding that the shoe-black was the owner of the dog, he taxed him with the artifice and after a little hesitation he confessed that he had taught the dog the trick in order to procure customers for himself.

Sligo Champion, 11 June 1836

OUT OF POCKET BOB-A-JOB DOG

The following anecdote of a dog, given in the *Sportsman's Annual,* is one of the most curious we have seen of its kind:— A gentleman of Suffolk being on an excursion with his friend, and having a Newfoundland dog soon became the subject of conversation; when the master, after a warm eulogium upon his perfections, assured his companion that he would, upon receiving the order, return, and fetch any article he should leave behind, from any distance.

To confirm this assertion, a marked shilling was put under a large square stone on the side of the road – being first shown to the dog. The gentlemen then rode for three miles, when the dog received his signal from the master to return for the shilling he had seen put under the stone. The dog turned back, the gentlemen rode on and reached home, but to their surprise and disappointment, the hitherto faithful messenger did not return during the day.

It afterwards appeared that [it] had gone to the place where the shilling was deposited, but the stone being too large for his strength to remove, he had stayed howling at the place, till two horsemen, riding by, and attracted by his seeming distress, stopped to look at him, when one of them alighting, removed the stone, and seeing the shilling, put it into his pocket, not at the time conceiving it to be the object of the dog's search.

The dog followed their horses for 20 miles, remained undisturbed in the room where they supped, followed the chambermaid into the bedchamber; and secreted himself under one of the beds. The possessor of the shilling hung his trousers upon a nail by the bedside, but when the travellers were both asleep, the dog took them in his mouth, and, leaping out of the window, which was left open on account of the sultry heat, reached the house of his master at four o'clock in the morning, with the prize he had made free with; in the pocket of which were found a watch and money, that were returned upon being advertised, when the whole mystery was mutually unravelled; to the admiration of all the parties.

The Odd Fellow, 2 November 1839

UNBEARABLY CURIOUS ADVENTURE

A very extraordinary circumstance is related of a young man that emigrated from Hampshire to the United States. It seems that the youth, accompanied by a middle-aged man, was travelling through some thick woods, when he espied a very large tree, on the branches of which appeared a path-way to the top; being struck with its appearance, his curiosity prompted him to ascend its summit, which had been previously broken off, and displayed a yawning hollow trunk.

After having viewed it, he was about to descend, when, by some accident, he missed his footing, and fell into the trunk, at the bottom of which lay two young bears. Here, he remained for some time before the man had courage to search for him and when he did, he was unable to render him any assistance. He went, however, to find a rope.

During his absence the old bear came; and what must have been the sensations of the unfortunate youth on seeing the huge body of the ferocious animal darkening in its descent his dreary habitation, which he might then literally consider his coffin.

The nature of the place, however, rendered it necessary for his frightful neighbour to descend with her tail foremost, as otherwise she could not have returned. Finding her in this posture, his only remedy, he thought, was to lay fast hold of her posterior, which so affrighted the bear that she immediately ascended, dragging him to the top, and her fear was so great that she fell off a branch and was killed, while the other quietly descended, to the great satisfaction of his companion, whom he met returning with assistance.

Northampton Mercury, 7 August 1841

CAT PUSSY-FOOTING AROUND WITH PUPPY

In our last [edition] we recorded the singular circumstance of a colt being suckled by a cow, and we now record an equally strange affair. Benjamin Estcourt of the Cross-Post Turnpike has a spaniel pup being reared by a cat: when it was taken from its mother it could not lap, and puss took compassion on it, and adopted it as one of her own progeny, and continues to show equal regard to it.

Cork Examiner, 30 August 1841

HAWKING POLITICAL OPINION

"On Friday last," says the *Tyne Mercury,* "two gentlemen tourists witnessed a severe conflict between four Martin swallows and five common sparrows in the air, near the road between Ardoch and Crieff. They fought nearly five minutes, when a hawk darted in amongst them; but no sooner was he recognized by them, than both parties uniting, encountered him, and beat him so severely that he was scarcely able to fly off with his life.

How happily this typifies the present conflict for place between the two great Parliamentary parties! The Martin swallows and sparrows are the Whigs and Tories and the hawk who darts in among them, clamorous for food, is the People; but no sooner do the contending parties recognize this new-comer, than they both unite to punish him severely for his impertinent intrusion, inasmuch as their quarrel *has nothing whatever to do with him,* but regards only their own self-interests!

Dundee Courier, 22 October 1844

FELINE FASHION CATASTROPHE

Last week an elderly female, residing in one of the manufacturing lanes of our city, had the misfortune to lose her favourite cat, which pined and died. Although she had still another three of the same species, she was almost inconsolable. She took to pieces a muslin or dimity petticoat and made a death-dress for the deceased, face-cloth and all, put her house every way in the order common among the people of her class when any of the inmates die, got candles and sat up all night watching the corpse. She performed the offices of sepulture to the dead animal early in the morning, and the three surviving cats appeared with black crape collars during the day.

The Bath Chronicle and Weekly Gazette, 24 April 1851

IF ONLY MICHAEL FISH HAD LEACHED OFF THIS INVENTION HIS FORECAST WOULD'VE BEEN A BREEZE

Among the articles in the *Great Exhibition* [1851] is a circular pyramidal apparatus three feet [0.91 metres] in diameter, and three feet six inches height [1.06 metres], composed of French-polished mahogany, silver and brass, to illustrate the discovery of Dr. Merryweather, of the means of anticipating storms, and which that gentleman has designated *The Tempest Prognosticator*. The well known influence of the electrical state of the atmosphere on the movements of the leech suggested Dr. Merryweather's apparatus, and forms the principle of its operation.

It consists of 12 bottles, each containing leeches and having a metallic tube of a particular form inserted in the neck, into which would be somewhat difficult for a leech to enter, but which it would make every effort to enter if a storm were preparing. In order to ascertain when the leeches have entered the tubes, when the person in charge is absent, or in the night time, there is a sort of mouse-trap arrangement of the tubes, formed by a small piece of whalebone, through which, when influenced by the electro-magnetic state of the atmosphere, the leeches would pass, and in doing which they would dislodge the whalebone and cause a bell to ring, and a register to be made of the operation.

The inventor states that the apparatus will communicate at all times the processes which are taking place at the higher regions of the atmosphere, and for hundreds of miles in extent will foretell with unerring certainty when any storm is about to take place. He also states that he could cause a little leech to ring St. Paul's [Cathedral] great bell as a signal for an approaching storm.

Leeds Intelligencer, 23 July 1853

UNPLEASANT PHEASANT BREAK-IN

The Gloucester Journal relates that Mr. Joyner Ellis, of Berkeley, has been obliged to have his sitting-room windows glazed with thick plate glass, in consequence of pheasants breaking them. Mrs. Ellis and family were in the habit of feeding the wild pheasants, which grew so tame that they used to tap at the window in the morning for their breakfast with such force that when the windows were glazed with ordinary glass they broke all the bottom panes, and fearlessly entered to pick up the crumbs under the table.

UN-BULL-IEVABLE – WHERE'S SIMON COWELL WHEN YOU NEED HIM?

A "performing bull" is being exhibited at the Alhambra Circus, Leicester Square, London. The beast jumps over hurdles and through hoops, lies down at the word of command, walks on his knees, and finally allows himself to be carried out of the ring in triumph on the shoulders of a number of men.

THIS MEAL WON'T BE A DOG'S DINNER – HE'S JUST HAD A WHEELY HARD DAY

[The turnspit dog was a long-bodied, short-legged dog bred to run on a wheel which turned meat over a cooking fire. The breed is now extinct].

Just as the invention of the spinning-jenny abolished the use of distaff [tools used in spinning] and wheel, so the invention of automaton roasting-jacks has destroyed the occupation of the turnspit dog, and by degrees has almost annihilated its very existence. Here and there a solitary turnspit may be seen, just as a spinning-wheel or distaff may be seen in a few isolated cottages; but both the dog and the implement are exceptions to the general rule, and are only worthy of notice as being curious relics of a bygone time.

In former days, and even within the remembrance of the present generation, the task of roasting a joint of meat or a fowl was a comparatively serious one, and required the constant attendance of the cook, in order to prevent its being spoiled by the unequal action of the fire.

The smoke-jack as it was rather improperly termed – inasmuch as it was turned, not by the smoke, but by the heated air which rushed up through the chimney – was a great improvement, because the spit revolved at a rate that corresponded with the heat of the fire. So complicated an apparatus, however, could not be applied to all chimneys, or in all localities, and therefore the services of the turnspit dog were brought into requisition.

At one extremity of the spit was fastened a large circular box, or hollow wheel, something like the wire wheels which are so often appended to squirrel-cages; and in this wheel the dog was accustomed to perform its daily task, by keeping it continually working. As the labour would be too great for a single dog, it was usual to keep at least two animals for the purpose, and to make them relieve each other at regular intervals. There are one or two varieties of this dog, but the true turnspit breed is now nearly extinct in this country.

Middlesex Chronicle, 8 June 1867

MASS MURDER ON UNPRECEDENTED SCALE

According to a Swiss journal a means has been discovered of making use of cockchafers. The *Estafette* of Lausanne states that between four and five million of these insects were sent to Freiburg for the manufacture of gas, and the residue forms an excellent carriage grease.

Dunfermline Saturday Press, 10 August 1867

REPTILLIAN CUISINE

A striped snake, 9 feet [2.74 metres] long, has been killed at Essex, Massachusetts, and in his inside were found four toads, three small turtles, four birds, and a large assortment of frogs, bugs, and other delicacies.

Edinburgh Evening News, 8 February 1875

TAIL OF A CRUSTACEAN TO WARM THE COCKLES OF YOUR HEART

A journalist met with a strange pet the other day when paying a visit. Whilst he was talking he noticed something moving on the carpet, which was neither dog nor cat. On looking again he saw that it was a fine lobster, dark grey, spotted with red, and thought that it must have escaped from the kitchen.

The lady of the house smiled, and said, "I must tell you the history of my pet. Some months ago I bought a lobster and as it was not wanted for my dinner my cook left it in water in the kitchen. I was going to a ball that night, and being ready sat on an easy chair, and fell fast asleep.

Suddenly I sprung up from a sharp bite on my foot, and saw the lobster biting it. I started up and ran to the kitchen. No-one was there and a cloth in front of the fire had caught fire. It was extinguished, but I have kept the lobster ever since out of gratitude."

It has its basin of cold water, and seems to recognise its mistress, and is so fond of music that it is always drawn towards the piano whenever she plays.

Illustrated Police News, 22 January 1876

PAWS FOR THOUGHT ABOUT MAN'S BEST FRIEND

Tax report of the Royal Zoological Society of Ireland, presented to the members of the 44th annual meeting, held in Dublin, states that "during the year the Gardens sustained a heavy loss in the death of the beautiful lioness, familiarly called 'old girl'. She was born in the Gardens, of South African stock, on September 1, 1859, and died on October 7, 1875, after six weeks of prostration from chronic bronchitis.

During her long and honoured career she presented the Gardens with 54 cubs, of which she actually reared 50, losing only four. This is a feat unprecedented in the annals of menageries and gardens.

The closing weeks of her useful life were marked by a touching incident worthy of being recorded. The carnivores when in health have no objection to the presence of rats in their cages; on the contrary, they rather welcome them as a relief to the monotony of existence, which constitutes the chief trial of a wild animal in confinement.

Thus, it is a common sight to see half-a-dozen rats gnawing the bones off which the lions have dined, while the satisfied carnivores look on contentedly, giving the poor rats an occasional wink with their sleepy eyes. In illness the case is different, for the ungrateful rats being able to nibble the toes of the lord of the forest before his death, and add considerably to his discomfort.

To save our lioness from this annoyance, we placed in her cage a fine little tan terrier, who was at first received with a sulky growl; but when the first rat appeared, and the lioness saw the little dog toss him into the air, catching him with professional skill across the loins with a snap as he came down, she began to understand what the terrier was for; she coaxed him to her side, folded her paws around him, and each night the little creature slept at the breast of the lioness enfolded within her paws, and watching that his natural enemies did not disturb the rest of his mistress. The rats therefore had a bad time during those six weeks.

Cornishman, 8 August 1878

LUGS FOR THE LUGHOLES

A Lochleven eel will "charm" away deafness. At any rate, live eels are sent from the Scottish Lake to London to try the effect.

TALE OF A DOG DOGGEDLY PURSUING DINNER

Mdlle. Delacroix appeared at a police station in Paris the other day on a charge of stealing meat from a butcher's shop, and was induced to make a confession which implicated her not only in this charge, but also in that of having perverted to wrongful purposes the instinct and devotion of her dog.

She had, in effect, trained this faithful animal to make raids upon a butcher's shop in the neighbourhood, and abstract from there a piece of meat, which he duly brought to his mistress's lodgings, and which eventually served to provide her with her daily meal. The butcher in question had, on several occasions, missed from his shop certain pieces of beef and mutton, and had apparently determined to keep a sharp look-out, in the hope of catching the thief.

He was not a little surprised one day to see a large dog stealthily leap upon the dresser and abstract a nice looking joint, which might be of the value of about 10 francs. He lost no time, however, in giving chase to the thief, who, according to his custom, made for home, and deposited the booty at the foot of *Mdlle*. Delacroix.

The butcher waited a few moments and then made his appearance in the house, when he found the fair owner of the dog in the act of cutting the joint. No further evidence was required, and the commissary of police proceeded at once to arrest the woman. She did not give herself the trouble to make any defence, and is said to have readily admitted that she had for some time been accustomed to her marketing in this original and ingenious but reprehensible fashion.

MISTAKEN IDENTITY ERROR OF JUMBO PROPORTIONS

A remarkable incident took place at the Scarborough Aquarium yesterday, the particulars which are vouched for by eye-witnesses. Among those present at the noon day performance of the elephant, Sheriff, was Mr Philburn, a detective in the police force. Philburn, owing to facial disfigurement, bore strong resemblance to Sheriff's former keeper, against whom the animal bears some resentment, and who had been dispensed with for Sheriff's original keeper (who has now charge of the animal).

On Sheriff advancing in Mr Philburn's direction it evidently at once perceived the resemblance, and bellowing and accelerating its speed, knocked Mr Philburn down. He was conveyed to the Leeds Hotel, and Dr. Cross was summoned. Mr Philburn has sustained internal injuries of a somewhat serious nature.

Portsmouth Evening News, 25 May 1893

THE CHATTERING CLASSES

Talking Monkeys. Professor Garner, who went out to Africa to study monkey language, says he has had extraordinary success. "I am safe on the coast," writes Professor Garner, "the proud possessor of a chimpanzee that can say, *'Tenakoe Paketa'*, which is Maori for 'good day, stranger'; a gorilla that knows 20 words of Fijian; and a female orang-utan that has picked up *'Donner und blitzen'* from my German valet, and has, judging from her actions, quite fallen in love with him. I have also got written down, which is more important, nearly 200 monkey words. The monkey language is a very primitive language. There are, perhaps, not more than 20 or 30 words in it that I have not already got, so that task is now practically completed."

THE LION KING BECOMES PART
OF THE AUDIENCE

The lion Wallace was being exhibited in the Clark Street Museum, the cage having been placed on the stage, and the trainer at his post. The trainer closed the door of the cage, as he thought, when he entered, but some obstacle prevented its fastening. The animal saw his opportunity and took advantage of it. He sprang through the door into the orchestra. The place was crowded, and there was a general stampede. The lion roared, and trotted up the centre aisle, while the people climbed upon the window-sills or made for the doors. The trainer followed the animal, promptly whipped him into subjection, and got him back to the cage.

THE BEAR, THE BICYCLE, AND THE BLOOMERS

Bruin does not object to bicycles in principle, but his indignation rises to striking point when he sees bloomers superimposed thereon. He rightly regards them, says the *Telegraph*, as successful competitors with his own ungainliness.

This was amusingly illustrated in Clapham Road, where a collision took place between a performing bear and a lady on a bike. Bruin was trudging quietly along and allowed to pass without observation by several women, wearing the orthodox skirts, on bicycles and tricycles.

At last, not far from Kennington Church a corpulent lady in bloomers came slowly wheeling along, and the moment he saw her, the bear suddenly snarled, jerked the chain out of his keeper's hand, and made for the bicyclist.

With his head he butted the machine, which, with the lady on it, fell over on himself, to the great amusement of a large number of spectators. The keeper promptly ran after his charge, and rescued him from underneath the frightened wheelwoman, who shrieked much, but was not wounded. He marched off the animal in haste once more, while the lady summoned a four-wheeler, put the damaged bicycle on the top, and drove off inside.

Yorkshire Evening Post, 2 June 1898

TAKE A FISH OUT OF WATER...

The Danger Of Sudden Changes. A scientist tells that there seems to be a peculiar fatality among fishes. After reaching a certain depth of water the swimming bladders become distended by the pressure of air, and the fish literally explode. Too much of one's native element may bring about most disastrous consequences.

A sudden change of air from one density to another may cause the rupture of a blood-vessel, and too sudden a change of temperature has produced like results. Extremes of all sorts are not only very injurious, but are likely to prove fatal, especially to organisms that are not in the enjoyment of robust health.

Sunderland Daily Echo and Shipping Gazette, 11 August 1903

CELL MATES OF MICE AND MEN

Among the many instances of prisoners who have sought to enlighten their captivity by making pets of birds or small animals, caught or lured within their cells, the case of William Johnson, a well-known south London character, stands out as unique.

Once upon a time, it would appear, William, during one of his periodical sojourns within the walls of Pentonville Gaol, made friends with a mouse by the simple but effective plan of sharing with it his "skilly" [thin porridge or soup] and his "toke" [tobacco].

So attached did he become to his pet that, when in due course his sentence expired, and he was ejected from his cell to make room for another lawbreaker, he carried it with him to freedom and the Borough slums. Here, however, neither food nor drink was to be had for the asking, and man and mouse might conceivably have perished for lack of nourishment, had not William journeyed to Bow Street Police Court and poured the story of his woes and those of his four-footed friend into the ears of the sitting magistrate.

The papers, as William had doubtless shrewdly foreseen, published the details of the case far and wide. And, as a result, a large number of charitable people forwarded money to relieve his – and his mouse's – necessities. Altogether the sums received amounted to £60.

It is a fact that many, even among the most abandoned ruffians, exhibit a love for and power over the lower animals that at times almost verges on the uncanny. Another convict had by some mysterious means induced a blackbird to follow him about the quarries while he was at work. This particular man was undergoing life sentence for the murder of his sweetheart, and it was recalled, a remarkable fact, that after committing the crime, he had returned to the room where the body lay for the purpose of releasing a thrush belonging to the dead girl, so that it might not die of starvation.

The man who first exhibited a troupe of performing fleas in public was an old convict, who learned in the loneliness of his cell how much these parasites are capable of when carefully trained. He realised a small fortune from his discovery and, forsaking the paths of crime, lived to a good old age, and died in the odour of sanctity.

Spiders, too, are constantly being made pets of by prisoners, and exhibit remarkable sagacity under careful training. "Big Harry" [Pascalis Caludis, ringleader of the mutiny on board the vessel *Lennie* sailing from Antwerp to New Orleans in 1875 in which the Captain, first and second mate were murdered], when in Newgate awaiting execution, used to feed a spider with flies, and talk to it, until it became so tame that it would at once answer to his call.

This same man, too, had a pet sparrow, which used to perch outside his cell window and peck crumbs from his outstretched hand. As he used a considerable quantity of his meagre ration of bread in this way, and as, moreover, he declined to touch meat owing to religious scruples, his warder exerted his influence to get him a small extra allowance.

"Big Harry" was exceedingly grateful for this, and, to show his gratitude, on the night before his execution, he made a model of his pet sparrow, and presented it to the warder. The bird was represented pecking a flower, the whole being manufactured out of the crumb of loaf made into paste. The flowers had berries, also broad, fixed stems made from the fibre drawn from the stuffing of his mattress, and the bird's legs were a couple of teeth broken off his comb.

Luton Times and Advertiser, 15 January 1904

A PET SHEEP JAMMIN' ALONG WITH THE WEED

A 10-year-old pet sheep, an orphan from Mr. C. Claridge's farm Heath, has "passed away". For a decade this petted animal has followed members of the family about house and grounds and village roads with cats and dogs as companions. It fared well on cake and beans, partook freely of any human food except meat, and had a special liking for such delicacies as jam and tobacco.

Bath Chronicle and Weekly Gazette, 27 December 1913

A PRIMA MATIE CASE

Remarkable Claim. £4,000 Demanded For Death Of Educated Monkey. A [law] suit for £4,000 has been entered against the city of Calgary, Alberta, by the owners of an educated monkey which died recently. The animal was being exhibited at a vaudeville theatre in that city. It appears that the monkey was being transported from the railway station to the theatre in question, when the wagon in which it was riding bumped over an obstruction of some kind in the street. The animal was thrown out on its head, and received injuries from which it died. The city refused to pay any compensation, with the result that the attorneys for the owners filed the suit for the amount stated.

BOA SAUSAGE AND TIGER PÂTÉS

Parisians are fond of eating strange foods for their Christmas Eve suppers, and this year they will eat mock tiger pâté or boa constrictor, in memory of the hunt for an escaped tiger at Eupernon recently, and the discovery of a boa constrictor in the Paris tube. Last year (says *The Express*) Paris ate, if not enjoyed, elephant steak, and the year before camel cutlets had considerable popularity.

MISSIVES AND MISSILES
FROM ACROSS THE GLOBE

HORRIBLE DISCOVERY OF HUMAN REMAINS

Ipswich Journal, 13 December 1729

WELL-BOORISH BEHAVIOUR

In the *Hague Courant* we see the following extraordinary occurrences, which had been all well attested before the Magistrates of Leeuwarden, by several eye-witnesses, viz. "That on the 12th of October last, some labourers being busy making a well for a Boor [farmer] in East Friesland [Netherlands], and having digged 24 feet [7.31 metres] deep, they heard a very great noise, which continued all the morning, and as they were boring the earth five or six foot [1.52 – 1.82 metres] deeper there issued out, to their great surprise, a sort of flame of fire, two or three times, which obliged them to cease their labour, and to refuse working again; however, all being still, the Boor prevailed on them to go down again into the well, which being done, the noise increased, and they expecting every moment the water to spring up with force, got up with all the speed they could, but before they were quite out, they heard a noise like the firing of a pistol, and some flames ascending, which singed and burned the labourers, in such a manner, that they were forced to keep to their beds for several weeks. The Boor's daughter looking down the well was also scorched. These flames continued several minutes, till at last, the water came pouring up, and put an end to them and the noise likewise.

Leeds Intelligencer, 2 July 1754

FIGHTING FORM FAILS TO SET WORLD ON FIRE

Bassano [in the region of Veneto, northern Italy], June 7. Of late we have had a remarkable phenomenon in these parts formed by inflamed vapours which arise from the Earth in the night, and fall into the shape of fiery balls, some rising to a man's height, and some gliding along the surface of the ground. This phenomenon has been oftener seen at the village of Loria and its neighbourhood, than in other parts of the country, and gives the peasants no small uneasiness, as the igneous vapours sometimes set their barns and stables on fire.

They put in practice every method they can think of to dissipate those ambulate fiery globes, sometimes throwing stones at them, and sometimes striking them with halberds, scythes, and other weapons.

Berkshire Chronicle, 5 March 1825

ANYONE FOR NOSE-PEGS WITH THEIR JELLY?

Among the greatest delicacies of Oonalashka [in the Aleutian Islands in present-day Alaska], says Captain Otto von Kotzebue, are the webbed feet of a seal, which are tied in a bladder, buried in the ground, and remain there till they are changed into a stinking jelly.

Bath Chronicle and Weekly Gazette, 6 October 1825

EXCLUSIVE – (POSSIBLY) THE WORLD'S FIRST SIGN OF GLOBAL WARMING

Letter to the Publisher from St Thomas, West Jamaica: We have had a very wet spring, which kept the crops back. It commenced with a very singular phenomenon, viz a shower of ice and hail: I picked up one piece which measured an inch in diameter, and half an inch in thickness. The oldest inhabitant never remembered the like before. The poor Negroes were terribly alarmed, and some of them said it was hot like fire, and that God Almighty had sent it to punish them.

DON'T DO AS I DO, DO AS I PREACH

The Africans are now, it seems, able to requite the kind exertions which we have so long made to diffuse the truths of Christianity among them, by sending missionaries in turn to this country. A black man has lately been preaching several times in Aylesbury and its neighbourhood: he says that before his arrival in England he had no idea that the people of this country, who sent missionaries to foreign countries to convert the natives to Christianity, were themselves addicted to swearing, drunkenness and all kinds of vice.

Bath Chronicle and Weekly Gazette, 14 January 1830

CARPING ON ABOUT HOW TO
GET A PIKE PICKLED

A discovery of great importance to the followers of *Epicurns* has been made by a French adept in the art of Good Living. It is the secret of sending carp and pike alive to any distance. The recipe is as follows: Steep the crumb of new bread in brandy, and when it is sufficiently swollen, fill the mouth of the fish with it, and afterwards pour in a small quantity of brandy. Wrap up the fish afterwards in fresh straw, secured with pack-thread, and cover the whole with a linen cloth. When the fish reaches its destination, let it be unpacked, and thrown into a tub of water, where it will remain a quarter or half an hour without giving any signs of life but at the expiration of that time, it will disgorge itself copiously, and resume its ordinary motions.

Northampton Mercury, 7 August 1841

OH BROTHER – SURPRISE, SURPRISE!

The Hague papers give the following painful account of the death of Madame Rochussen, the young and amiable wife of the Dutch Minister of Finance [Jan Jacob , later to become Prime Minister of The Netherlands 1858-1860]: She had lain in a few weeks ago, but was still in a feeble state, when her brother, whom she had not seen for 10 years, arrived from abroad.

Intending to give his sister an agreeable surprise he entered her chamber without even her knowing that he was in Holland. The shock was so strong that Madame Rochussen was thrown into a fainting fit, which terminated in her death, before even the Minister could be called from his cabinet to receive her last sigh.

Stamford Mercury, 17 November 1854

BATTLE OF BALAKLAVA – GRAVE TACTICS OF WAR

It is said that the Russian Governor sent in yesterday (23rd October) to Lord Raglan to ask for a day's truce to bury the dead on both sides. The same authority has it that Lord Raglan replied he had "no dead to bury".

The Russians in revenge for this are leaving their dead where they fall outside the lines, and also bring them out from the town and place them in the valley frequented by our pickets and skirmishers, who are much annoyed by the stench. This is a new engine of warfare.

The Western Times, 2 June 1855

GETTING CARRIED AWAY OVER AN UNSCIENTIFIC EXPERIMENT

An attempt to ascertain the depth of the Niagara river, above the Falls, has failed. A mass of metal, weighing 40 pounds [18.14 kgs], attached to a line, was dropped from the high railway bridge; it sank for a few moments, but was quickly borne forward by the impetuous current, and was seen some distance down the river on the surface – the rush of water prevented it from sinking.

Norfolk Chronicle, 23 August 1856

NOT RIFLING THEIR WAY INTO THE LOCALS' AFFECTIONS

A party of American gentlemen, travelling recently to Egypt, and feeling disposed for a little rifle practice, actually made target of the Sphinx.

Dunfermline Saturday Press, 10 August 1867

PLATFORM TO SUCCESS BUT THIRD-CLASS PASSENGERS HAVE FARTHER TO FALL

The Strasbourg line of railway has just introduced a new carriage. It is, in fact, a three-storey carriage. The ground floor is the first-class; the second-class is *au second*, and third above. It is a great saving of space, and on that line the bridges, etc, are high enough allow these new carriages to pass.

HOLY HORRORS

The Inquisition, or "Holy Office" as it is termed, is of a very early date. Its history can be traced through succeeding centuries. Inquisitions were appointed as far back as the year 382, and about the year 800 the power of the western bishops was enlarged and courts were established for trying and punishing spiritual offenders, even with death; the punishment being termed in Spain "An act of faith".

Nearly 3,000 persons were burnt in Andalusia, in addition to 17,000 who suffered other penalties in the year 1481. This dreadful tribunal was finally abolished by the Cortes in 1813. [Spanish historian Juan Antonio] Llorente states that in 236 years the total amount in Spain of persons put to death by the Inquisition was about 32,000; 291,000 were subjected to other punishments.

We are reminded of these facts by a strange circumstance which took place but a few days since. An immense quantity of human remains has been discovered in the hollow walls of one of the wards of the old San Andreas Hospital, at Lima. Between 4,000 and 5,000 skeletons have been counted, and it is supposed that the bones belong to victims of the Inquisition.

Cornishman, 8 August 1878

OILING THE WHEELS OF THE WITCHCRAFT INDUSTRY

In Bonny [a realm in what is now Nigeria], Africa, the natives have been bewailing the death of the wife of 'Captain' Harts, a leading chief. For nine days heavy guns were discharged in rapid succession in her honour, upwards of 500 kegs of gunpowder being consumed for the purpose. Superstition still being universally prevalent, the "Grand Ju-ju" [witchcraft] was made in order to bring the deceased lady to life. This failing, 100 puncheons [barrels] of oil were offered to anyone who should accomplish the feat.

Aberdeen Evening Express, 20 January 1879

BUGGED TO DEATH BY AN EXORCISM

The French Government had offered some time since a reward of 300,000L [livre] for a remedy for the phylloxera, or vine-bug. About as many cures were naturally handed in, but only one – the use of sulphuret of carbon – has come up to the standard of "perfect".

The Univers, the chief Ultramontane journal, publishes its remedy – an exorcism, without bell, book, or candle light, employed with efficacy in 1584 when vines, be it remarked, *en passant*, were strangers to phylloxera and oidium. It is only necessary for the clergyman to recite the prayer around the field, and the noxious insects will at once disappear. In Ireland St Patrick gave the toads and frogs a twist, and banished all the serpents. The exorcism is equally good against slugs, snails, and locusts; it is capital against toads and rats, whose bodies will be found on the soil like autumn leaves. One trial is enough.

Aberdeen Evening Express, 9 July 1889

A CAT-ASTROPHIC DELUSION

The "Woman Cat", says a Paris telegram, who has just escaped from the Salpetriere Hospital forms a frequent topic of sensational talk and conjecture just now. It appears that last week a good-looking and apparently healthy girl of 15 was taken to the hospital by her friends. She was examined by Dr Parinand, and while he was looking at her eyes she suddenly went on all fours, her features became distorted, her eyes glared, and imitating the mewing of a cat, she endeavoured to bite the persons who were standing near her.

After having acted for several moments in this manner, the patient began to lick her hands, and then gradually returned to her senses. When under examination by Dr Charcot, the girl had another attack of her malady, and she bit the eminent surgeon severely in the leg. Charcot had hopes of curing the patient, but she has suddenly disappeared from the Salpetriere and is now wandering at large through Paris.

Birmingham Daily Post, 10 January 1891

CLUBBING NEW YORK STYLE

Every "clubbable" man [in New York] belongs to half a dozen or more clubs. In no other city in the world are there so many little clubs, or so many different varieties. There is a class of men – it perhaps numbers 700 or 800 – which may be safely counted upon as eager to join almost any new organisation of the sort; and the natural outcome of the whole situation is that the New York clubs, besides being numerous, are in many cases of a very novel and eccentric character.

There is for instance the *Tenderloin*. Tenderloin is the nickname of a district of rather unsavoury reputation between Fourteenth and Forty-second Streets... in the heart of it, established in a tumbledown wooden shanty, which was once known as the "Eel Pot", is the *Tenderloin Club*.

It was formerly a haunt of thieves; it now numbers among its members some of the most distinguished authors, artists, musicians, doctors and lawyers in the city; but it still retains many of the internal characteristics of a thieves' kitchen. The floors are sanded or saw-dusted; the furniture is rude in the extreme; and there is an ostentatious absence of comfort. Elsewhere there is a ghastly museum, composed almost entirely of lethal weapons, each one of which has killed its man. Many of these fearsome relics were contributed by the New York police.

The Thirteen Club, being a somewhat older organisation, is better known. It dines at 13 minutes past the hour on the 13th day of every month, with 13 people at each table, 13 courses, 13 toasts, 13 candles, and 13 coffin-shaped wine-lists; and it has 1,300 members.

Even madder and more eccentric is the *Owl Club*, which consists of exactly 365 members each one of whom has a distinctive title – as, for example Chief Owl, Dry Owl, Key Owl, and so on. The Chief Owl presides, using as his chairman's hammer a gilded ham-bone.

The *Last Man's Club*, the *Tough Club*, the *Sudden Death Club*, the *Sewer Club* and the *Pot-Luck Club* are other eccentric clubs of New York. Of them, however, the present writer has, unfortunately, no personal knowledge.

The *Ichthyophagous Club* contains its eccentricities to dining solely on fish, and to eating fish – including sharks, devil-fish, octopods, jelly-fish, star-fish, and limpets – that is not usually sent to civilised tables.

Last on the list comes the *Peanut Club*. The qualifications for this organisation do not appear to be strictly defined; but it is required that every member shall upon all occasions carry about with him some kind of specimen of the humble peanut.

Portsmouth Evening News, 25 May 1893

TOUCH OF SPICE FOR THE BOYS IN INDIA
LOOKING FOR HOT STUFF

A few days since startling details were published as to the alleged State regulation of vice in India. The disclosures were of such a shocking character as to appear almost incredible, and the public were relieved a day or two later by a statement from General [Frederick Sleigh] Roberts [Commander-in-Chief in India], to the effect that, as he knew nothing of the matter, the story could not be true.

True or not, however, the details were repeated last night before a public meeting by Mrs. Andrews, one of the ladies charged with the investigation. She declared, on the authority of some of the unfortunate women themselves, that the Government built their houses, and that they were paid as wages 10 rupees a month, while in each house Mrs. Andrews declared she found a watchman in Government uniform.

She further alleged that they saw the 50th West Kent Regiment, "the lads had only been out a month, but 14 tents of vice had been erected for them". It is clear that the matter cannot be allowed to rest where it is; an official inquiry will have to be instituted, and the sooner it takes place the better.

Liverpool Echo, 8 July 1893

BREMEN POLEAXED BY BERLIN OVER POOR POLES

It is possible to be "too smart" and clever in one's dealings, and the community of Bremen are finding this fact out. The discovery arose in this way. About a couple of years ago someone posted up placards in various districts of Russian Poland stating that a Polish kingdom would be established in Brazil, and inviting the natives of the district to emigrate to that country.

Brazil's evil reputation had apparently not reached this part of Poland, for great numbers went to Bremen, where they were by the placard told that they would receive free passage to the promised new Kingdom of Poland. At Bremen, however, they met with disappointment, for it turned out that the whole affair was a hoax. There was no free passage, and there was no new Poland across the Atlantic.

Under the circumstances the would-be colonists did exactly what might be expected of people of their condition and imperfect education, they turned their steps to the inns of the place, of which they took possession, with a view of drowning their sorrows in the flowing bowl. In this they were so successful that before they left the inns they had spent their last silver and were quite destitute.

There was, of course, nothing left but to appeal to the Bremen authorities for assistance, but they failed to see the necessity for supporting a large body of Poles, and so engaging a special train they got the people to board (there were about 1,000 in all), and sent them on to Berlin, telling them that the train would take them straight to Brazil.

This exercise of smartness, however, landed the Bremen authorities in the law courts, and a couple days back the Berlin Poorlaw Board gained a judicial authority empowering them to recover the expenses of sending the Poles back to their homes from the Bremen Board.

One cannot demur to this decision of the court, for the authorities were undoubtedly guilty of harshness (to put it mildly) in sending those poor people to a distant city regardless of the sufferings which would be entailed on them during the journey. What, however, can be said of the authors of this hoax, by which some scores, if not some hundreds, of the unfortunate victims have been ruined?

NO BURNING DESIRE SO IDEA OF MARRIAGE BLOSSOMS

Orchid-hunting leads to strange adventures. M. Hamelin, the collector who has sent home all the specimens of the *Eulophiella Elizabethae* that have hitherto reached these shores, narrates in a letter how he won a dusky bride, and moreover secured his preserves of the famous plant from all poaching on the part of brother depredators – or, more euphemistically, plant-collectors. While searching the woods of Madagascar he had for guide and hunter the brother of the chief, Mayombosa. This unhappy guide had the misfortune to be so severely mauled by a Madagascar lion that he died, and M. Hamelin returned alone to tell the tale. After the recital the irate chief gave the survivor the option of marrying the widow or being greased and burnt. He chose the lesser of two evils, but coupled with the marriage contract an undertaking on the part of his brother-in-law to close those lands to all other orchid-seekers.

Daily Gazette for Middlesbrough, 13 July 1893

YOUNG ZULU RISES TO GREAT HEIGHTS

The following description is given of a marvellous exhibition by a Zulu witch doctor witnessed by the writer. The performance took place at night in the light of a fire. Having put a young Zulu into a trance-like condition, the witch doctor turned to the high grass a few feet behind, and gathered a handful of stalks about 8ft [2.43 metres] long.

Standing in the shadow and away from the fire, he waved with a swift motion the bunch of grass around the head of the young Zulu, who lay as dead in the firelight. In a moment or two the grass seemed to ignite in its flight, although the witch doctor was not standing within 20 feet [6.09 metres] of the fire, and burned slowly, cracking audibly.

Approaching more closely the form of the native in the trance, the conjurer waved the flaming grass gently over his figure, about a foot [0.30 metres] from the flesh. To my intense amazement the recumbent body slowly rose from the ground and floated upward in the air to a height about 3 feet [0.91 metres], remaining in suspension and moving up and down, according as the passes of the burning grass were slower or faster.

As the grass burned out and dropped to the ground, the body returned to its position on the ground, and after a few passes from the hand of the witch doctor, the young Zulu leaped to his feet, apparently none the worse for his wonderful experience.

CHARITY FUNDRAISER KISSED INTO TOUCH

A novelty was introduced at a bazaar in Cincinnati on Saturday. Several ladies to the number of some dozens volunteered to be hugged and kissed by any man who chose to pay for the privilege. A tariff was drawn up – 10 cents for an unmarried lady, 15 cents for a married lady, and 25 cents for a widow.

The men had to blindfolded. One of the blindfolded men, John Reynolds, paid 15 cents, and, approaching the married women, caught hold of one right before him and led her out and kissed and hugged her most boisterously, and evidently enjoyed himself immensely.

When the bandage was removed from his eyes he found that the lady locked in his arms was his wife. Furiously, he demanded his money back, and, this being refused, smashed some of the furniture, kicked over several tables on which goods were displayed for sale, and behaved like a maniac. Then the police were called in and it took two of them to subdue him.

BURNING DESIRE TO MARRY BEFORE
GOING OFF THE RAILS

An eloping couple in Tennessee were married on Saturday in one of the strangest places yet recorded as the scene of a wedding. Mr W.A. Cagill and Miss S. A. Lyle, of Knoxville, finding their parents obdurate, determined to run away, and boarded a train on the Knoxville and Augusta Railway.

Meeting a friend on the train, they confided their plight to him. He told them that the fireman on the locomotive, T. H. Hodge, was a Justice of the Peace. The fireman was interviewed at the first stop, and consented to tie the knot at the next station. The young people hastened to the locomotive, and climbed into the cab, where the fireman-magistrate, all grimy and greasy, and attired in his overalls, stood on the foot-plate, and spoke the few words necessary to marry them. Then the bride and groom ran back to their car, the whistle blew, and they were off on their honeymoon.

Luton Times and Advertiser, 15 January 1904

HAMMING IT UP AT A BALD-HEADED CLUB

A bizarre club has just been formed at Fribourg, in Switzerland. The only qualification for membership is a bald head. The rules set forth that the members must meet every month in order to eat ham and listen to music!

Western Times, 25 May 1906

HOW THE TIMES HAVE CHANGED!

It has been our exceeding privilege to have had as Ambassadors from the United States a succession of men not only eminent in the world of letters, but who have fitted in to our social life, and departed from us with deep regret on both sides. This reflection is suggested by the fact that Mr. Whitelaw Reid, the new Ambassador, very graciously presided at the annual dinner of the Newspaper Press Fund (one of the finest benevolent organisations in our midst), and made a very interesting speech on British journalism.

Mr. Whitelaw was quite at home, for he is a thorough newspaper man. Beginning life as reporter, he has ended as proprietor of the giant *New York Tribune*, and as representative of the Republic at the Court of St. James.

It is flattering to us to have the assurance of Mr. Reid that he admires the solidity, the good credit, the respectability, and the responsibility of the English Press, and he made this significant remark, "If you knew more of the Press that you do not have, you would, perhaps, have a greater appreciation of the Press that you have." His Excellency warned against the adoption of American slang – a warning that is needed, though it must, to the credit of our more responsible journals, be said that they have rigidly adhered to English pure and undefiled.

CRIME AND PUNISHMENT

Leeds Intelligencer, 2 July 1754

NO OSCAR AWARDS FOR THESE DISARMING DUMB-DUMBS

Yesterday three men and a woman received a flogging at the whipping post here, for endeavouring to impose the most notorious falsehoods on our Magistrates, which afterwards they confessed were so. One of the men had, or pretended to have, no tongue; another had really but one arm, and the third had a withered left-hand. This is mentioned to caution the charitably credulous not to be imposed on by such daring imposters, one of whom threatened to fire the town. They had women and children belonging to the gang to the amount of above 20.

Ipswich Journal, 19 October 1771

CHINESE WATER TORTURE

Extract of a letter from a gentleman at Canton in China to his friend in London: It is astonishing the rigour with which all the Europeans are treated here, who in the smallest degree transgress any of their laws. An officer belonging to one of our ships was going down from this place to where they lie, and in passing one of their custom-houses, was called by some of the Mandarins to stop in order to be examined, a custom they observe by all boats passing up and down the river with Europeans in them.

The officer happened to be in a great hurry, he was running before the tide with all his sails crowded, and as he was a considerable way past, he thought it was unnecessary to put back; however, they alarmed some of their armed boats that were ahead, a number of these collected themselves, when a scuffle ensued.

The officer was somewhat obstinate, and ordered the men to stand upon their defence, thinking to get clear, but not by any means to fire, for they were all armed, unless there was an absolute necessity. The boats came close round, and some of the Chinese attempted to board them; upon which one of the seamen, being in liquor, fired without orders, and wounded an inferior Mandarin; upon this they were crowded upon by intense numbers, and the officer thought it most prudent to deliver himself and his men without further bloodshed or aggravation of their crime, as in that case death must have been inevitable to them all immediately, it being impossible to effect an escape from such a multitude.

They were brought up to Canton, and condemned to be exposed in an open boat, without being suffered to have any covering over their heads, to shield them from the violence of the meridian sun, or copious dew which fell in the night, for three weeks.

This was put in execution; they were all soon seized with violent fevers, and in about 10 days every man of them died. There were six men, besides the second officer of the ship to which they belong. In the mean time all stop was put to trafficking with the English, which lasted for upwards of three months, to the great detriment of our shipping.

Chester Courant , 7 October 1794

A CLERICAL ERROR BOUND TO MISFIRE

A Rev. Mr Jones has actually published, in the *Ipswich Journal,* a proposal for arming the clergy!

Leeds Mercury, 31 January 1807

ASLEEP ON THE JOB

The game in the manor of Boynton, Carnaby & Co, belonging to Sir Geo. Strickland, having of late been destroyed by a set of poachers, in order to detect them a nightly watch has been kept; and early on the morning of Friday last week the gamekeeper, along with other servants, walking in an avenue adjoining a plantation, heard a person snoring; they immediately proceeded to the place from whence the sound came, and found two fellows asleep, having beside them a bag containing nine hares, two rabbits, and two pheasants: also a loaded gun: the men were secured and had before Ralph Creyke, Esq, and committed to a Beverley House of Correction.

Bath Chronicle and Weekly Gazette, 3 February 1825

NOTHING SWEET ABOUT 500 LASHES

Storey, convicted of forgery at Demerara [former British colony now part of Guyana] has received his sentence which was 500 lashes under the gallows, with the rope around his neck, and seven years imprisonment with hard labour.

Liverpool Mercury, 26 August 1842

HELPING TO CLEAR A DINNER TABLE

On Monday evening last most of the lodges of the *Independent Order of Odd Fellows* had a dinner in their various club-rooms. There was one at Mrs Knott's public house, Whitechapel, and Mary Ormsby, the wife of one of the members, was in the lodge room. She was seen to put a tumbler down her breast, and on being examined, just as she was about to leave the house, two other tumblers, with a knife and spoon, were found in her pocket. She was given into custody and on Tuesday sent to gaol for one month.

PULPIT SERMON IS A PITFALL TOO FAR FOR PIT-STRIKERS

How to beat the turn-outs. The Lancashire mob [part of the 1842 General Strike] sent word the other day to Leeds that they meant to sleep on Wednesday night in the parish church of that town. It is said that the vicar of Leeds sent for answer, that if they did come to the church he should be in the pulpit, and would assuredly preach to them all night. This threat had the desired effect.

Leicestershire Mercury, 22 April 1843

MILLER WORKS HIS FINGERS TO THE BONE

We have heard that an extensive seizure has lately been made in London of flour belonging to a Kentish miller, with which a great quantity of bone dust was mixed, and that the party in question has been heavily fined.

Dundee Courier, 22 October 1844

ALL'S WELL THAT ENDS WELL

On the afternoon of Friday last, a party left the Chapelshade [Dundee] with the intention of interring the body of a still-born child. After proceeding to some distance, however, the mourners had got tired of their labours and the father, a person of the name of Nicoll, and a companion named Rollo, after enjoying themselves at several public houses, began to consider that there was no necessity for putting themselves to the trouble of internment, and agreed to throw the body into a well at the Hawkhill, which they accordingly did. It was, however, discovered on Saturday and taken to the Police Office; and after some inquiry the father was found out. Yesterday he was permitted to take away the body, and this time we believe it got decent interment at Logie Kirk Yard.

London Daily News, 29 December 1847

REVENGE FEARS BLOWN UP OUT OF ALL PROPORTION?

Lawyers are in the habit of being "blown up" metaphorically by the press, but they may be allowed to protest against attempts to blow them up literally by powder. A new gunpowder plot is currently reported by the "studious Templars'" to be just now in preparation against them and their tenements.

Respectable and studious barristers who "eschew delights and love laborious days," even at Christmas time, sedentary convey-ancers, chamber-bound under press of papers, and painful pleaders detained from the festivities of the season by the unseasonable benevolence of clients, were twice last week put in bodily fear by the subaqueous proceedings of some explosive experimenters on the Thames in front of the Temple gardens.

It is no exaggeration to say that the buildings "reeled," from base-ment to attic, under these alarming concussions. Remonstrances poured in to the Treasury – affrighted clerks were scuttling up and down staircases – learned opinions were suspended – and counsel, buried in the perusal of reports indoors, jumped up, in the fear of being buried, from the effects of reports out-of-doors. The only explanation that could be got at was, that "somebody was blowing up something on the river".

The two reports, which had convulsed the stability of the building, and the peace of mind of its occupants, are preliminary, it is said, to a grand explosion to come off this week. Since this information was given, it is noticed that departures for the country have been unusually numerous from the disturbed districts of the Temple, or, in other words, the courts adjoining the river.

The Burnley Advertiser, 3 January 1857

A BIRD-BRAINED IDEA LEADS TO FASHION MOST FOWL

A fashionably-dressed young lady was recently seized at the Paris Barriers, and under her crinoline, which was of ample dimensions, was found a gigantic turkey, tied by its head to her stays [corset].

Worcestershire Chronicle, 30 November 1859

A DEVILISHLY FEARFUL JOB THAT'S TOO HOT TO HANDLE

The Rev. E. H. Beckles, rector of St. Peter's, in the island of Antigua, has been appointed Bishop of the fatal diocese of Sierra Leone. He is the fourth bishop within seven years; his three predecessors have been killed by the climate.

Portsmouth Evening News, 1 January 1878

A PERSIAN CARPETING

If justice in Persia is not effective it is not because an error is made on the side of mercy. The English courier of the British Legation was recently robbed, being mistaken for a post office messenger, and as the theft appeared to be the result of a conspiracy involving a number people, the authorities thought it necessary to subject the persons arrested to severe punishment. The right hand of each was cut off at the wrist, and the wrist was thereupon steeped in boiling oil to prevent excessive bleeding. After that the right hand was tied to the left wrist, and the thieves were led in this state through the public bazaar, where they were compelled to solicit presents for the executioner. This punishment, it is said, was intended a warning to others. It ought to be.

Western Daily Press, 23 April 1878

THE FAILED SWEENEY TODD IN A LITTLE SHOP OF HORRORS

A murder of very extraordinary character, with a minimum of motive and the certainty of immediate detection, was perpetrated on Saturday in the Rue St. Lazare, Paris. A collector of the Societe Générale was walking along the Rue St. Lazare at 8 o'clock in the morning when the owner of a curiosity shop, at No. 50, named Martin, to whom he was a total stranger, called after him and asked if he would be good enough to change a note of 1,000 francs.

Although against the rules the collector, whose name was Sebalte, consented to oblige the shopkeeper. He had a good deal of money about him and counted out nearly 1,000 francs while Martin went into a back parlour to look, he said, for the note. But he returned with the stump of a sword, which he plunged at once into the breast of his good-natured visitor.

Sebalte staggered to the door, cried out "I am assassinated," and drawing from the wound the scrap of the weapon, fell dead on the pavement. Martin ran away, but was arrested at the corner of the Rue Taitbout. It seems that he took the shop three months ago and paid a quarter's rent in advance. Being pressed for the second quarter, just come due, he said he would pay in the course of the day.

Martin has since confessed his crime to the Judge of Instruction. He says he wanted money to pay his rent, and, having noticed that many collecting clerks went by his house at an early hour, the idea struck him that by killing one he might get out of his difficulty. He had a trapdoor of his cellar ready open to conceal the body, and, had his victim fallen dead at once, as he ferociously calculated, instead of staggering into the street, the cutting up of the corpse and its gradual disappearance would have been very possible.

Pall Mall Gazette, 16 January 1879

YOU'D HAVE TO BE TOTALLY PLASTERED TO ENJOY THIS PARIS-STYLE BREAD

The meeting of the City Commission of Sewers last week was enlivened by the exhibition of a model of a donkey's head, made from Plaster of Paris extracted by Dr Saunders, the medical officer of health and public analyst, from some adulterated or spurious flour lately seized by him in his official capacity under the provisions of the Nuisances Removal Act, 1863. The "meal" thus seized was contained in 79 sacks at Lower Thames Street. An application made to the Lord Mayor to have the flour condemned was refused, Dr Saunders alleges, in no courteous terms; and he asked the Court for further instructions, observing that the matter pressed for early action, as some of the flour had been sold to a foreign baker in Soho, who had made from it 114 "wheaten" loaves of bread, two samples of which he had laid, with the model of the donkey's head, upon the table of the Court. It was decided, after some discussion, to order fresh proceedings be taken at once before the Lord Mayor, with the object of getting the flour condemned and it is most sincerely to be hoped that no legal difficulties will prevent their success.

Aberdeen Evening Express, 20 January 1879

SECRET SERVICES RUSSIAN OUT EXCUSES

A London correspondent writes: "It is greatly to be hoped that the Russian police are not going to saddle us unfortunate Londoners with any more murderers at large. We have quite enough of our own, the perpetrator of the Burton Crescent crime [murder of elderly widow and boarding house owner Mrs Rachel Samuels] being now added to the list.

The story goes that the Czar [Alexander II] is extremely displeased with his secret police for not discovering the murderers of General Mezentzoff [Chief of the Imperial regime's secret police in the Third Section]; and, by way of "fixing" them somewhere, the police declare that they have escaped to England, and are lurking in the environs of London. Our criminal investigators had better return the compliment, and say that the Burton Crescent murderer is hiding in St Petersburg.

MOST REMARKABLY GOOD BEHAVIOUR

An extraordinary story reaches us from Princetown [Dartmoor], details of which are only known within the boundaries of the convict settlement, and which have hitherto been kept secret. A few days ago a party of about 25 convicts were on marches, as is their custom, out into the bogs, some distance from the prison itself, and two miles from the village of Princetown. They were in the charge of a warder who had only just been added to the prison staff.

Whilst occupied at their labours one of the convicts suddenly stooped and picked up some large stones, which he threw at the warder. One of them struck him behind the ear, and felled him insensible to the ground. The loaded rifle which he carried fell from his hands, and the convicts then made a rush towards the warder for the purpose of maltreating him.

A convict named Stevens, who had only recently arrived at Princetown, seeing the danger to which the warder was exposed, outstripped the other convicts, and arriving first, stopped and picked up the loaded rifle, together with the pouch of ammunition carried by the helpless man. Standing astride his form this convict fired at his advancing comrades, winging five or six of them by shooting them in the legs. His ammunition exhausted, the convict then changed ends with the rifle and knocked over about an equal number, some of the wounds inflicted being of a shocking character.

Stevens stands over six feet [1.82 metres] and is powerful in proportion. The force of his blows was tremendous. By this time the warders, who at a distance surrounded the working party of convicts had closed in, and Stevens on their arrival threw down his rifle and explained what had occurred. A number of carts were obtained to convey the injured convicts to the Prison Infirmary. The remainder were handcuffed and escorted to the prison.

Stevens received the commendation of the Governor, and

was placed in a cell in a different portion of the establishment, away from the others. Stevens was called up by the Governor and informed by him that in consequence of his courageous conduct the Home Secretary had ordered him to be released and rewarded. Stevens was so overcome he sobbed like a child. The sentence he was serving was transportation for life; he had only served 12 months.

Sheffield Evening Telegraph, 23 December 1887

SOUNDS FAMILIAR… WAS THIS CRIME SOLVED BY INSPECTOR KNACKER OF THE YARD?

At Nottingham today John Jonson was charged with depositing a quantity of putrid beef, brawn, and sausages for sale. It was proved that the prisoner rented the cellar wherein was found the putrid flesh and a sausage machine. He obtained a large quantity of horse flesh from knackers' yards, chopped it in with the putrid beef, and made sausages of it, which were sold by other men. Two hundred pounds [90.7 kgs] weight of unwholesome meat was discovered in the cellar. He was sentenced to three months' hard labour.

Illustrated Police News, 11 December 1897

LADIES RAPIER TONGUE-LASHINGS

A Ladies' Duel. Madrid. December 4. Our correspondent writes: Great laxity of morals is prevalent here; duelling, bull-fighting, and assassination being by no means uncommon. At the present moment Madrid is in a state of great excitement in anticipation of a duel between the notorious mistress of Senor Donvaldez and the well-known Spanish dancer, Carmen Paxadol. The quarrel arose by the former lady throwing a bundle of onions on the stage during the latter's performance.

The result of this insult was a 'challenge to fight a duel with rapiers' on the field of honour. Our correspondent succeeded in gaining an interview with Madrid's famous dancer at the San Franco Academy of Fencing, and to his inquiries received the following reply: "The duel will take place shortly, but I must not tell you where, as I do not wish the *gendarmes* [policemen] to interrupt the combat. I am in deadly earnest, and nothing but a blood-stained rapier will satisfy my sense of honour."

With these dramatic words the hero of the forthcoming battle led the way to the gymnasium, where several fair fencers were trying their skill. Thanks to the courtesy of Senor Lorenzo, the able fencing instructor, our correspondent was permitted to take a photograph of the Academy of Fencing and its interesting members. The lady with the sash round her waist is Carmen Paxadol, the subject of this interview [see image on page 137].

Illustrated Police News, 5 February 1898

BELLE OF THE BALL'S QUICK-FIRE RESPONSE TO FOOT-IN-MOUTH YOUTH

An extraordinary shooting affair took place the other night at Keystone, West Virginia. During a dance at a ball an awkward country youth accidentally trod on the foot of a girl of unusually good looks, and the acknowledged belle of the ball. She called upon him to apologise, but he declined, as he was unconscious of having touched her foot. She thereupon whipped a revolver out of her pocket and shot him dead. She was promptly arrested and placed in gaol, but says she is glad she shot him. The town is greatly excited over the murder. Many persons believe that the rudeness of the youth was not the real cause of the shooting.

SALACIOUS GOSSIP,
SCANDAL AND SCALLYWAGS

Ipswich Journal, 19 October 1771

20-YEAR-OLD ABANDONED AFTER ELOPING WITH HUSBAND'S COUSIN

[General Scott was a politician and celebrated gambler who apparently enjoyed phenomenal luck. It is said that he won the hand of his first wife, Lady Mary, in settlement of a gambling debt owing to him by her father James, the Earl of Errol.]

Some further particulars of *The Northern Couple* are come to hand, viz. that Lady Mary S. [Scott] who is daughter to the E—l of E _____ [Earl of Errol], is about 20, and the General [John Scott] about 45; that on his marriage he settled 1,500 pounds per annum on her, and 100,000 pounds on the children that should be their issue; that she has bore him one child which is dead; that the Captain [James Sutherland] is second cousin to the General, and owes his education and commission to the General, who had placed him in his own regiment, and admitted him to his table; but on perceiving a whispering intimacy between the imprudent parties, he recommended, and at last insisted, that the Captain should join his regiment; this brought on the elopement, which was thus executed: the General had company, whom he entertained genteelly; as soon as they were gone he went to bed, and My Lady said she would follow, but soon after decamped with her gallant in a tim-whisky [one-horse carriage].

In the morning the General missed his Lady, sent for a clergyman and a counsellor, and with them he pursued the runaways, who bent their course for London in a post-chaise and pair [carriage and two horses], whilst the General pursued in a chaise and four; at Barnet the Lady was fatigued and it was agreed she should go to bed.

Her servant was bade to call the Captain at five in the morning, but at three up comes the General, seizes the baggage that was in the camp, and her servant that guarded it, who soon confessed all he knew, and with a candle in his hand called up the Captain, saying it was five o'clock. The Captain came to the door, saw the General with a pistol in his hand, clapt to the door and bolted it; and whilst the General was forcing the door, he jumped from the chamber into the stable-yard, and made off [it is said without so much as a rag on him].

The General sent his friends into the Lady's room, and left them to take care of her, himself coming to London, and from his house sent a maid-servant to wait on her mistress, to her father's in the north. The Lady had brought off her jewels, and the Captain had in his pocket about 50 pounds in cash, and a 20 pound bank note, with which it was designed they should go off to France. A suit is said to be already commenced in Doctor's Commons [a society of lawyers] against Lady Mary S---- and Captain S _____ d, for criminal conduct.

Oxford Journal , 19 October 1771

TITTLE-TATTLE

Certain advices have been received from Paris, which say that the King of Spain has actually insisted on the co-operation of the Court of France with him in a scheme to be put in motion early the ensuing spring; and in case of non-compliance, threatened to dissolve the Alliance now subsisting between the two Crowns. Lewis [King Louis XV] was greatly alarmed at this, and forced to take his head out of the bosom of his fair Enchantress [Madame Du Barry], and betake himself to study. A Council was summoned, when it was determined to favour the demands of his Catholic Majesty. Since this, every method has been taken to drain money from the Subjects, and some of the most oppressive kind that ever was attempted in that Kingdom before.

Ipswich Journal, 23 October 1784

WED-LOCKED IN SHAME AND MISERY

A curious marriage was lately celebrated in Drury Lane, which strongly marks the progress of folly and dissipation. A man of some considerable fortune was kept for a week in a bagnio [brothel] in a state of intoxication, and became so infatuated as to propose immediate marriage to one of the most common prostitutes of the place. Care was taken that he should be kept as devoid of reason as possible, until the business was finished, which was done with all the splendour of Old Drury.

He gave a grand dinner to the Mother Abbess, and as many nuns as she pleased to invite – and thus a gentleman, who perhaps deserved a better fate, was hurried by intoxication and proportioned infatuation, into a life of shame and misery. Let the youth of spirit and intrigue read this, and learn to avoid those haunts, and that company, where, the ambition is, to level all to the same standard of unhappiness, and delude human nature by the corrupt influence of its dregs.

The British Chronicle, or, *Pugh's Hereford Journal,* 15 September 1790

WHAT A CARRY ON! IT'S TIT FOR TAT – THE VALET'S REVENGE

The following circumstances created some buzz at a fashionable watering place last Tuesday night. Lord xxx, who had possessed a tenderness for the wife of his valet for some considerable time past, at length managed matters so well as to effect an appointment for passing the above night with her, and to that purpose previously sent her husband away to a town some miles distant, upon business which would have detained him until the next day. Thomas, however, suspecting the fidelity of his wife, put off his journey and concealed himself in an apartment adjoining his wife's.

At the hour of assignation his Lordship quitted his Lady, and repaired to Mrs Anne; Thomas then shifted from his lurking place and having the key of his wife's room in his pocket, when he found all quiet, very deliberately locked up the Peer with his *enamorata*, and then repaired to his Lady's chamber, where he filled the place his Lordship had resigned. In the morning, gentle readers, you may picture to yourselves the confusion of the whole family; his Lordship was found locked in the arms of Mrs Anne and her Ladyship was discovered in the same situation with Mr Thomas.

London Daily News, 3 January 1850

WAS THIS LOVER THREE SHEETS TO THE WIND?

Great excitement prevailed in the Rue de la Harpe [Paris] early on Saturday morning, by pieces of furniture, crockery, sheets, blankets, etc, being thrown from a window on the fifth story. On going to the room, the landlord to his great surprise found lying on the floor and bawling lustily, a young man fastened in a sheet. All the neighbours hastened to the spot, but it was some time before any explanation of the late extraordinary affair could be given. It at length appeared that the young man, a student, had not paid for his furniture, and that the upholsterer threatened to take it away; that this greatly exasperated his mistress, who resolved to be revenged in the morning on the upholsterer; and that accordingly she rose calmly, sewed her lover tightly in a sheet, and then set to work to smash and tear everything, and throw it out of the window.

The Star, 12 February 1885

FIRED-UP ANGRY MAJOR MAKES MAJOR MISTAKE

A Major of the Hussars, in the service of Austria, was paying a visit at a certain castle on the borders of Hungary, the Lord of which was about to give a magnificent entertainment worthy of his own rank and the splendid castle he inhabited.

The guests were numerous, and when the arrangements for the night were made, it was found that it would be impossible to accommodate all of them in the castle unless someone would consent to sleep in one of the rooms which bore the reputation of being haunted.

The veteran Major, who was remarkable for his bravery, which he had proved on many a battlefield, gladly undertook to occupy the room, and having partaken of the evening's festivities, retired after 12 o'clock, having given public warning that it would be very dangerous to play any trick on him; an intimation which no-one doubted his ability and willingness to act up to. The Major, after having carefully loaded his pistols, laid them on the table by his bedside, and, leaving the candle burning, went to bed. He had not slept more than an hour when he was awakened by a strain of mournful music.

Three ladies dressed in an antique costume of green appeared at the lower end of the room, who sang in solemn tones a requiem. The Major listened for some time to the mournful notes of the dirge; at length he called out, "Ladies, this is very well, but somewhat monotonous – will you be so kind as to change the tune?"

The ladies still continued singing the death-hymn, despite the Major's remonstrances, and he began to grow angry. "Ladies," he said, "I must consider this as a trick for the purpose of frightening me, and as I regard it as an impertinence, I shall take a rough mode of stopping it." He thereupon took up his pistols, but the ladies still sang on. The Major, by this time seriously angry, said, "I shall wait but five minutes, after that I shall fire without hesitation."

The five minutes elapsed; "I still give you, ladies," he said," while I count 20." He counted one, two, three, accordingly; but on getting to the higher numbers, and repeating once more his intention to fire, the numbers 17 – 18 – 19 were pronounced with long pauses between, and a solemn assurance that the pistols were cocked.

As he said the word 20 he fired both pistols at the singers – but the fairy music still went on! The Major was so startled that he was confined to his bed by a severe illness, for more than three weeks.

The trick had been accomplished by a concave mirror which threw the reflection of the ladies in green, who were really in an adjoining room, into the Major's room, so that he only fired at their shadows.

Carlisle Journal, 4 January 1856

WASHERWOMAN COMES CLEAN OVER DIRTY DUKE AFFAIR

Rumours, widely circulated and extensively believed, assert that a young Duke, bearing one of the most celebrated historical titles of France, was found murdered upon the bridge of Asniéres, the other evening. He had entered into an intrigue with a washerwoman, whose husband, in the rage of a surprise, stabbed the ducal paramour of his wife, and chased him undressed until he fell dying upon the bridge. *Figaro* is the only Paris journal which has alluded to the event. The allusion is truly French, advising young noblemen, when they choose their mistresses, not to choose, like M. de N—, their laundress.

British good sense sends about town, and into families, women of a certain age as laundresses, while the Parisian washerwomen are the youngest, prettiest, freshest, the most tempting, and most tempted girls in this debauched metropolis.

Judging from his portrait, which I have seen in the shop windows, the Duc de N-- was one of the handsomest young fellows of his time. No jury would convict as an assassin the husband, who was in the right, according to French morality, opinion, and law; and the family of the noble Duke will not prosecute, to avoid scandal, and to conceal his pitiful end.

Worcestershire Chronicle, 30 November 1859

ONE MUST BASH ON WITH ONE'S GRAND TOUR

On the 6th of July Mr. Allcock, the English consul-general to Japan, landed at Shinagawa, accompanied by his wife, who attracted the Japanese more than all the rest of the party, she being the first European lady that, ever stepped foot on Jeddo [Edo, Japan] soil, and to them, with her crinoline spread out, and gaily trimmed bonnet, she was an object of considerable attraction, and was eyed by all the crowd, who would run ahead of her so as to look her in the face; some of them took hold of parts of her dress, and this ungentlemanly conduct she very properly resented by giving them smart raps over their heads with her parasol.

Dunfermline Saturday Press, 10 August 1867

WONDERS WILL NEVER CEASE

A remarkable marriage was solemnised in Dundee last week. The principal actors in the affair were an old man, of stature not exceeding 4 and a half feet [1.37 metres], whose age is 96, and a smart spruce-looking damsel of 28.

Bolton Evening News, 12 March 1869

OLDER HUSBAND CAST ASIDE FOR YOUNG MAN

The Glasgow Herald of yesterday says: "A most extraordinary piece of scandal in high life has come to light, namely, the elopement of the wife of Captain Vivian with the Marquis of Waterford. The gallant Captain is Lord of the Treasury, and Member Parliament for Truro. The runaway wife (she is the Captain's second wife) is Florence, daughter of the late Major Rowley, Bombay cavalry. The whereabouts of the runaway pair has not yet been traded, but Captain Vivian is in full pursuit. The Captain is in his 61st year; the lady much younger. The Marquis is 25.

Illustrated Police News, 4 August 1883

BOUQUET OF FLOUR AT A WEDDING

Mary Kearns, a young married woman, has been charged at the Cleator Moor (Cumberland) petty sessions with doing wilful damage to a hat and jacket, the property of Bernard Murphy, and also with assaulting Jane Murphy, his wife.

Bernard was a young man of 25, and his wife an old lady apparently not far off 70, and the two were only married a day or two since, the alleged assault taking place at the wedding. Kearns was the step-daughter of Mrs. Murphy by her first husband, who only died in November last, leaving all his property to his wife.

This caused ill-feeling between Mrs. Murphy and her stepdaughter, and a large crowd assembled at the wedding and hooted the pair. Mrs. Kearns, as they came out of church, struck the bride with a flour bag, completely spoiling her hat and jacket, to which a good deal of the flour, which was wet, adhered. Her face and clothing were completely covered with the flour, and the Rev. Father Wray, who married them, had to take the bride into his own house to divest herself of her outer garments. The crowd continued the demonstrations at the house of the couple in the evening.

The case was dismissed on a legal point, the summonses being taken out in the name of the husband, whereas according to the new Married Woman's Property Act they should have been taken out by the wife herself, to whom the damaged clothing belonged.

Edinburgh Evening News, 28 May 1886

A FRUITFUL RECEPTION MORE EFFECTIVE THAN A FROSTY ONE

A grocer named Mariner, of Lake Road, Portsmouth, who had recently retired and passed the business to his son, lost his wife last March (two months previously). On Wednesday the man, who is between 50 and 60, married a Miss Lock, who was 16 years old last Christmas, and was formerly a domestic servant in his employment.

To show their contempt for his conduct the neighbours put up mourning shutters and hung out bows of crape. A crowd collected, and when two wedding carriages with postillions [drivers] drove up to take away the couple, damaged fruit, onions, and other missiles were freely thrown. The man's son also put up mourning shutters, and just before the wedding party left, he drove off with a handsome wreath to place upon the grave of his mother.

Sheffield Evening Telegraph, 23 December 1887

ABSENCE OF BELLS RINGS IN THE CHANGES TO END ORGIES

Christmas Orgies At Limerick. "Terrible Saturnalia". The Roman Catholic clergy of Limerick are, a correspondent says, making a strong effort to prevent on Christmas Eve a renewal of the orgies which the lower classes of the population in that city of both sexes have annually indulged from the moment the clock struck the midnight hour until an advanced hour on Christmas morning.

During a sermon this week Father O'Connell said it was the custom from time immemorial to hear the bells of St. Mary's Church and the several churches of the city welcome the great festival, and citizens used to remain up to hear the music of the chimes. The custom, began and carried for a good and holy purpose for so many years, had sunk into an outrageous sink of awful unspeakable degradation.

Drunkards roared and howled through the slums and in the principal streets all night long. Children of tender age appeared to take part in the terrible Saturnalia, and the tramp of thousands of feet of adults and children, of reeling old age and of shrieking women, forgetful of sex or decency, might be heard long after the bells had ceased to ring out their joyous notes for another and a sacred purpose. It became a public scandal, and to prevent a recurrence of the scene it is proposed that the bells shall not be rung, and that public-houses shall close early.

Dundee Advertiser, 11 October 1892

AN ALIEN LOVE ALIENATES THE BIG BOSS

Births and deaths, by despotic law (says the *Daily Chronicle*) are removed from the control even of Emperors, but if a Berlin telegram is to be believed, the German Emperor [Wilhelm II] reserves to himself the veto of some of his subjects' marriages. The latest from papers from the Far Fast have brought the news of the engagement of Herr von Brandt, the German Minister to China, to Miss Heard, the daughter of the American Minister to Korea, and as both the intending bride and bridegroom have host friends, congratulations have been plentiful.

But the potentate who "sits up aloft" at Potsdam has had his cold eye upon the happy pair, and, like a bolt from the blue, he is said to have dropped upon them the crushing dictum that the "position of a German diplomatist is such to preclude him marrying a woman of another nationality". Love laughs at locksmiths, we know; and we suspect the little god is able to elude Emperors as well. As a matter of fact, also, nothing is more common than for the diplomatist to avail himself of his unequalled opportunities for falling in love with "a woman of another nationality".

Daily Gazette for Middlesbrough, 13 July 1893

SENTENCED TO MATRIMONY

A young man and a young woman were contesting possession of a piece of property, the one claiming under an old lease, and the other claiming under an old will. "It strikes me," said the justice, "that there is a pleasant and easy way to terminate this law suit. The plaintiff seems to be a very respectable young man, and this is a very nice young woman. They can get married and live upon the farm. If they go on with the law proceedings, the property will be frittered away among the lawyers, who, I am sure, are not ungallant enough to wish this marriage should not take place." The lady blushed and the young man stammered that they "liked each other a little bit," so a verdict was rendered for the plaintiff on the condition of his promise to marry the defendant within two months – a stay of execution being put to the verdict till the marriage ceremony should be completed.

Yorkshire Evening Post, 24 March 1899

UPSTAIRS, DOWNSTAIRS, IN MY LADY'S CHAMBER

Countess Wyanoff, of St. Petersburg, has been married to her own footman. This handsome young fellow had long worshipped his mistress. One day the countess surprised him as he was impressing a passionate kiss on her photograph. Instead of scolding or punishing the audacious flunkey she threw her arms round his neck, kissed him, and assured him that his love was returned. Her marriage with the footman took place at Berne.

EXTRAORDINARY PEOPLE

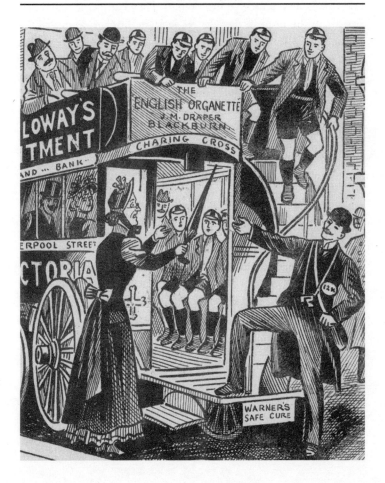

Oxford Journal , 19 October 1771

PLOUGHMAN'S LAST LUNCH

We hear from Shetland that one Andrew Tait died at North Yell (one of the Shetland Islands) in July last, aged about 120 years. He was in the service of a gentleman of that island as a ploughman in the year 1672.

Leeds Mercury, 31 January 1807

FOXY LADY

The following extraordinary circumstances have recently taken place in Dublin: A person who had served a most respectable family with zeal and fidelity as a manservant, for upwards of six years, was, on Friday last taken ill, and confined to bed.

A most unaccountable reluctance was evinced on the part of the person indisposed to admit the offices of a physician, until in alarming crisis in the disorder, induced the master of the family to insist on having recourse to medical advice, which however, there was not sufficient time to procure before honest *James* was delivered of a bouncing girl!

It is unnecessary to add until that moment that the real sex of this newly-discovered heroine had never been suspected. It is no less extraordinary that she was particularly adroit in attending on horses, and several times accompanied the gentleman of the family on severe fox chases.

Leicester Chronicle, 11 November 1854

BLACK LADY STRIKES THE QUEEN

The Mayence Journal contains the following, dated Aschaffenburg, 27th October, under the head of the "Black Lady," a pendant to the legendary "White Lady" of the Berlin Palace, whose apparition is believed to announce the approaching death of some member of the Hohenzollern family:

"The Queen Theresa of Bavaria [8 July 1792 – 26 October 1854] died of cholera at Munich, as already known. I hasten to communicate to your readers the following highly interesting and affecting details, of which I can guarantee the exact veracity:– On the 6th of October, between eight and nine o'clock in the evening, two princes of the Bavarian royal family, equal in birth and relationship, were seated at tea in a room of the Aschaffenburg Palace. A folding door divides this room from another apartment, and a smaller papered door separates it from the ante-chamber usually occupied by the domestics in waiting.

All of a sudden the latter door opened, and a lady covered with a black veil entered and made a low curtsey before the two illustrious personages. One of the princes, no little astounded, asked the lady if she were invited to tea, and, pointing to the folding door leading into the tea-room (where the Queen and ladies were assembled), gave her to understand that she should enter. No reply, and the lady vanished through the small papered door.

Both the illustrious personages were extremely agitated by this wonderful apparition and its mysterious disappearance. One of them immediately hastened to the ante-chamber to inquire of the servants about the mysterious figure. No one had seen it come or go, except Asvat, Queen Theresa's body hussar, who had met it in the passage. No other trace could be discovered. Both illustrious persons narrated what had occurred, and it soon came to Queen Theresa's ears, and she was so overwhelmed thereby that she became greatly indisposed, and wept during the whole night. The journey to Munich was fixed for the following day. All the luggage and half the servants were already on the road. To remain longer at Aschaffenburg was scarcely possible.

Queen Theresa was filled with the most sorrowful forebodings. She asked several times if it were not possible to remain here. It would be too painful for her to quit Aschaffenburg at this time. The mysterious and ominous Black Lady glided constantly before her imagination. Somewhat calmed, at length, by judicious observations, she at last sorrowfully commenced the journey, which it was not possible to postpone.

But still, at Munich, where she was at first lightly indisposed, but recovered, her mind was preoccupied with the apparition of the Black Lady, of whom she spoke to many persons with trembling apprehension. She was sought to be consoled by saying that the sentries on duty had seen the lady enter the Palace. But all was in vain. The idea that the apparition of the figure had a sinister foreboding for her life never quitted her mind. Twenty days after the mysterious evening, the Queen Theresa lay a corpse in the Wittelbacher Palace.

Your readers are at liberty to judge of the incident as you please. I must, however, solemnly protest against any suspicion being thrown upon the exact truth of these facts, derived verbatim from the statement of the best informed persons before I had the slightest suspicion of the Queen's death.

The two illustrious persons narrated the circumstance of the apparition minutely to several persons, so that the whole town heard of it next morning, and on the same evening the whole personnel of the palace and the soldiers on duty were strictly examined, and requested to state all they knew of the matter – a good proof that the occurrence cannot be set down among ordinary nursery tales."

The Carlisle Journal, 4 January 1856

CHARGE AGAINST THE LIGHT BRIGADE – WAR MAY BE TOUGH BUT THE FOOD'S EVEN TOUGHER TO SWALLOW

A lady's journal during the war. Messrs. Longman have just published a book entitled *A Journal kept during the Russian War: from the departure of the Army from England, in April, 1854, to the Fall of Sebastopol,* by Mrs. H. Duberly.

This lady set sail with her husband, an officer in the 8th Hussars, on the 24th of April, 1854. She sailed with the regiment to Scutari, and thence to Varna. Despite of Lord Raglan's prohibition, she smuggled herself on board one of the transports for the Crimea, went repeatedly on shore, but, instead of joining the army, went in the Star of the South to Balaclava, and remained on board until her husband could prepare a hut for her reception.

She was continually on shore, however, and may be said to have gone through all the dangers of the campaign, as she was rarely absent when fighting was going on. On the 20th of March last her hut was ready – she rejoined her Harry, and resumed camp life. There we part company with her at the end of September, three weeks after she had witnessed the great, final, and successful assault.

The circumstances in which she was placed led her often to express herself in a startling manner. For example, the Varna camp: "June 5th. Was awoke by the reveille at half-past two; rose, packed our bed and tent, got a stale egg and mouthful of brandy, and was in my saddle by half-past five."

Again: "A welcome sight presented itself in the shape of Captain Frazer and some bottles of beer, one of which I drank like a thirsty horse." In another place: "Our chicken was so tough that we could not get it down, even with the aid of our daily onions."

She was near at hand during the charge of the Light Brigade, and pictures it with a few touches: "I only know that I saw Captain Nolan galloping; that presently the Light Brigade, leaving their position, advanced by themselves, although in the face of the whole Russian force, and under a fire that seemed pouring from all sides, as though every bush was a musket, every stone in the hillside a gun. Faster and faster they rode. How we watched them! They are out of sight, but presently come a few horsemen, straggling, galloping back. What can those skirmishers be doing? See, they form together again. Good God! it is the Light Brigade."

Hereford Journal, 19 May 1866

LARGE AUDIENCE FOR LITTLE PEOPLE

[American little person Charles Stratton was exhibited in Europe by showman Phineas Taylor Barnum and was catapulted to international fame. After his wedding ceremony, such was Stratton's status, that he was received by President Lincoln at the White House.]

Advertisement: Shire Hall, Hereford. One day more, this Saturday, May 19. Three entertainments at 11, 3 and 8 o'clock. Wonderful combination! The world never saw the like! Patronised by Her Most Gracious Majesty the Queen, the Prince and Princess of Wales, the Royal Family, and most of the Crowned Heads of Europe.

The original and world-renowned Man Miniature, Charles S. Stratton, 31 inches [78.74 cms], known as General Tom Thumb and his celebrated little wife. Together with their infant daughter, the wonder of the age; and also the equally renowned Commodore Nutt, and the Infinitesimal Minnie Warren, the four smallest mature human beings ever known on the face of the globe.

The General, his wife, their infant daughter, Commodore Nutt, and Minnie Warren, are conveyed the same time in their miniature carriage to and from the Hall at each exhibition, drawn by two of the smallest ponies in the world. The public are respectfully informed that this will be positively the last appearance in this place of the General previous to his retiring into private life, which it is shortly his intention to do. At the Eleven o'clock Levee only do they appear in the identical costume as worn, by Command, before Her Most Gracious Majesty.

HARE TODAY, OFF ON A BROOMSTICK TOMORROW

Witchcraft In Dorset. Reports continue to be received of a remarkable case of superstition in the village of East Knighton in Dorset. The circumstances have been amongst the chief topics of discussion in all the countryside for weeks past. In a cottage dwells a woman named Kerley and her daughter, a girl of about 18. The latter is supposed to be bewitched – to be the subject of the strangest manifestations.

It is positively declared that articles have been thrown out of the cottage into the street, although neither window nor door was open, and these are stated to have been sent flying about in all directions. An old woman named Burt is set down as the cause of all this mischief, and she is declared to have assumed the form a hare, to have been chased by the neighbours, and then to have sat up and looked defiantly at them. It is positively believed that until blood is drawn from the witch the manifestations will not cease.

GERMAN SPIES AND THEIR ARTFUL DEVICES

The Paris correspondent of the *Daily News* telegraphs as follows: Major Blumenthal, an officer of the German Landwehr, has on suspicion of being a spy, been ordered leave France within 48 hours.

Suspicions were aroused by his taking, under the assumed name of Baron de Jilly, a chalet near Conflans, not far from Paris. A lady who was supposed to have taken a part of the chalet from him turns out have been a German military cadet.

They both used to go wandering about with a perambulator. What seemed to be a sleeping baby was in reality a large doll that had a photographic apparatus for taking views of the new forts and the positions commanding them. They were also enthusiastic pigeon fanciers, but some of their birds were trapped by suspicious neighbours, and found to be carriers.

Aberdeen Evening Express, 9 July 1889

CLERIC SHOULD'VE WORN A
CAT NOT DOG COLLAR

As far as it is known no species of bird is absolutely uneatable, at any rate none is poisonous. Once, when a lad, I stewed a jackdaw and, though the flesh was tough, the gravy was most savoury and tempting. Few four-footed animals are uneatable, and it is only among fishes and fruits that we find poisons.

My brother once brought me two squirrels which he had shot, and having read that gipsies relished them, we watched our opportunity, and in the absence of the family, set to work over the dining-room fire and stewed them; and I must confess that, whether it was owing to the share we had in preparing them, or to the omnivorous nature of the boys' appetites, we had no cause to complain that the dish lacked tenderness, flavour or wholesomeness; but I do not suggest that these charming little rodents should be slaughtered by way of general experiment.

Jugged cat I have not eaten, but a clergyman once told that me that he and some clerical friends, living in rooms together, were much tormented by the frequent visits of a clerical brother, who would drop in when least wanted, and was not satisfied unless a rich meal was forthwith prepared for his capacious appetite.

One day these young scrapegraces [incorrigible rascals] obtained a large cat which the cook most skillfully prepared for the delectation of the old clergyman who had been duly invited, thus forestalling one of his usual visits. Some excuse was made, and the old fellow, much to his joy, found himself the sole partaker of a large and delicious dish of hare, and he ate as only the rectorial appetite could eat. Never had he tasted anything so choice: the flavour, the tenderness, the gravy and the jelly were most tempting.

The sequel to the story is not, however, what I would wish. At last, when his appetite had been satisfied, one of his hosts began uttering cries like those of the cat, and after a little time the guest awoke to the startling consciousness that he had demolished a large cat.

He was almost at once taken ill, and for some days was in extreme danger. Whether that was due to the character of the meal or to the enormous quantity he had contrived to dispose of was never ascertained. He stoutly maintained the former, and his hosts the latter.

However that may be, the experience of the siege of Paris is conclusive that, in moderation, hardly any animal is unwholesome, for not only were horses, dogs and cats eaten when they be got, but hippopotami, elephants and mules.

Aberdeen Journal, 25 August 1890

PATENTLY PREPOSTEROUS

A contributor to the *New York World* has been amusing himself by rummaging among the specifications of new inventions stored in the Patent Office in Washington. Many of them are amusing, and some decidedly crazy.

The illuminated cat was granted a patent in 1884. It is a cat of pasteboard or tin for the purpose of frightening rats or mice. It is to be made in a sitting posture, and it is painted over with phosphorus so that it shines in the dark like a cat on fire.

Another cat, equally funny, is a patent sheet-iron animal, which is worked by clockwork, and has a bellows beside it which swells up its tail to the size of the maddest of Toms. If properly set, it will emit a noise equal to the wildest of midnight caterwaulers, and it has, in addition, steel claws and teeth. You wind it up, place it on your roof, and set it howling. All the cats in the neighbourhood jump for it and its poisoned claws kill everyone it strikes.

The patents to make women beautiful are numerous. The nose improver is one of the most curious of these patents. It has made, it is said, a fortune for its inventor, and it consists of a metal shell formed of two parts, which are connected by a hinge. The shape of its inside is that of a perfect nose, aquiline Roman or Grecian, as you prefer, and it does all its work at night.

The patent states that the nose should be first well bathed in warm water and then greased with olive oil until it is thoroughly softened. After this the improver is to be attached, and the person using it is to go to bed and sleep until morning.

At first, it is said, the operation is somewhat painful, but this wears off in a few nights, and the soft cartilage of the nose soon begins to assume the form of the beautiful shape of the improver. At the end of eight weeks you have a brand now nose, which remains with you until you get tired of it, when you buy a different style of improver and come out in a new nose quite different from your last one, but still beautiful.

Burnley Express, 3 October 1892

TENNYSON'S DEATH CAUSES DOCTOR'S PSEUDO-INTELLECTUAL POETIC LICENCE TO ERUPT

Alfred, Lord Tennyson, after a few days' illness, died at 1.30am on Thursday morning at Aldworth, near Haslemere. Sir Andrew Clarke, the famous physician, who was at the bedside of the distinguished poet, says: "Lord Tennyson has had a gloriously beautiful death. In all my experience I have never witnessed anything more glorious. There was no artificial light [in] the chamber, and all was darkness but for the silvery light of the moon at its full. The soft beams of light fell upon the bed and played upon the features of the dying poet like a halo of Rembrandt's."

Illustrated Police News, 31 October 1896

LADY'S SHOCK AS BOYS' KNEES EXPOSED ON OMNIBUS

On Wednesday afternoon there was an extraordinary scene in an omnibus near Victoria Station. Some boys representing a school football club in the West Central district had been a playing a match at Battersea. They wore their football knickers and stockings, covered in the majority of instances by long overcoats. The eldest boy in the team is 16 years of age, though some of them considerably less.

On returning to Victoria the bigger boys mounted to the roof of the bus, whilst two or three of the younger ones got inside. When the latter sat down they very naturally opened their overcoats, and about 4in [10.16cms] of leg and knee were exposed.

This was enough for a severe-looking lady seated in the corner of the bus. Screaming loudly she called upon the conductor to put a stop to what she called "such a gross and indecent exhibition", and at the same time she pointed to the knees of the poor little footballers, who evidently wondered what they bad done to excite such a commotion.

The conductor was a family man with boys of his own. He laughed loudly when the lady explained the situation to him, and stoutly refused to turn the boys out. "They hain't doin' any harm, ma'am, and I only wish everybody could show such good knees as them." Whether the lady took this to be a personal reflection or not will possibly never be known; but it is certain that she at once alighted from the omnibus, loudly declaring that she would call upon the National Vigilance Society to put a stop to such an exhibition of bare knees.

If this lady should happen to meet a Highland regiment in "full" dress the result would probably be fatal.

Shields Daily Gazette, 16 March 1903

THE ROYAL HOUSEWIFE AND ORIGINAL PEOPLE'S PRINCESS

Good stories, like good wine, are often stored long before being retailed. One story which is just being told of Her Majesty the Queen relates to an incident which occurred soon after the opening of the Alexandra Trust building in City Road, [London] EC.

As was stated at the time, Her Majesty, who was then, of course, Princess of Wales [Princess Alexandra], paid a surprise visit to the Trust, accompanied by the King, and to the astonishment and temporary embarrassment of the entire staff, sat down at one of the public tables and asked to be served with a three-course dinner for five pence.

The menu on that day consisted of soup, roast beef and vegetables, and Christmas pudding. The soup was brought and pronounced to be excellent. The roast beef and vegetables were then served, and these, too, their Majesties highly praised for their good quality. Then the pudding was placed on the table, and a portion was cut for Her Majesty, who tasted it and declared it delicious.

"But tell me," Her Majesty remarked, "do you always stone the raisins?" The official hesitated. "Not always," he replied, in evident confusion. "Well, these raisins have been stoned," quietly pursued the Royal and keenly observant housewife. "Was the pudding made specially for us?"

The official saw that it was useless to conceal the precise truth, and he therefore explained that the pudding and others had been made two or three weeks beforehand for a special occasion, but that the only difference was that the raisins were stoned.

"Then please take this away," said Her Majesty smiling, "and bring us the same kind of pudding that the people have." And the "people's pudding" was duly brought to the table and tasted by the Queen, who graciously remarked that it was extremely good, and congratulated the official on serving food of such high quality for the poor people.

Western Morning News, 14 January 1928

HARDY'S HEART FAR FROM THE MADDING CROWD

Dorchester, Friday. Mr. Thomas Hardy's heart will lie buried in the churchyard at Stinsford – the Mellstock of his novels – where his first wife and his father and mother were buried. The decision that Mr. Hardy should be buried in Westminster Abbey instead of in the Dorset he loved so deeply and made so famous caused considerable surprise to Dorchester people.

Miss Teresa Hardy, a cousin, said to today: "There is nothing in honours, and I think it is cruel that he should be buried in the Abbey, instead of among his own people, where he so much wanted to be buried." Mr. Henry Hardy, a brother, and Miss Kate Hardy, a sister, shared this view.

Rev. H. G. B. Cowley, rector of Stinsford, said: "I am very deeply disappointed by the decision, and I think Mr. Hardy's wish should have been respected. Of course, we all realize that it is a very great honour to Dorset and to literature that Mr. Hardy should have an Abbey burial." Mr. Cowley added that he had a letter from Mr. Hardy in his possession to the effect that he hoped to buried in Stinsford Church.

In view of the strength of local feeling that some part of Dorset's great writer should be buried in his native soil, and his memory not perpetuated merely by a tablet, Mr. Cowley approached Mrs. Hardy this afternoon with the suggestion that Mr. Hardy's heart should be buried in Stinsford Churchyard.

Mrs. Hardy, who is one the executors, immediately gave her glad consent, and an urgent telegram was sent to Mr. Cockerell, the literary executor, who is staying tonight in London with Sir James Barrie. At 7 o'clock this evening Mr. Cockerell telephoned his consent. Tonight the heart of the poet novelist will be removed [and was subsequently buried in the grave of his first wife, Emma].

The site of the burial place for Thomas Hardy has been selected in the Poets' Corner. It will be next to the tomb of Charles Dickens.

LIST OF ILLUSTRATIONS

Chapter 1, page 13: Death by tight-lacing of a fashionable corset. *Illustrated Police News*, 25 June 1870.

Chapter 2, page 41: A quack doctor selling his remedies on the streets of London. Wood engraving by E. L. Sambourne, *Punch*, 11 November 1893.

Chapter 3, page 55: The actress Sarah Bernhardt in her Paris studio. *The Graphic*, 5 July 1890.

Chapter 4, page 69: Chinese diplomat Li Hung Chang makes his way to England. *Western Mail*, 21 July 1900.

Chapter 5, page 87: Man takes donkey for a ride. *Illustrated Police News*, 22 January 1876.

Chapter 6, page 101: The Lion King plays with the orchestra. *Illustrated Police News*, 3 March 1894.

Chapter 7, page 121: Thousands of skeletons discovered in Lima hospital's walls. *Illustrated Police News*, 22 January 1876.

Chapter 8, page 137: Spanish ladies duelling for attention. *Illustrated Police News*, 11 December 1897.

Chapter 9, page 149: Bouquet of flour thrown at a bride. *Illustrated Police News*, 4 August 1883.

Chapter 10, page 161: Lady outraged by exposure of boys' knees. *Illustrated Police News*, 31 October 1896.

Also published by The British Library

The Finishing Touch
Cosmetics through the Ages

'The quest for physical beauty is essentially
as old as Woman herself.'
A Complete Guide to Personal Loveliness, 1937

In this fascinating book Julian Walker explores a curious, sometimes uncomfortable history of our age-old desire to look beautiful. He reveals dozens of the (occasionally desperate) ways in which people have tried to make themselves more attractive and alluring, and to hold back the ravages of time. The book tells a story of ingenuity and imagination, but also of self-delusion, trickery and exploitation.

The Finishing Touch celebrates enduring human vanity through an intriguing variety of materials and methods. Among the bizarre home remedies and grotesque commercial products featured are a facewash based on minced and boiled pigeons; hair conditioner made from bears' grease; a recipe for horseradish stirred into sour milk to lighten a tan; an Anglo-Saxon prescription for cosmetic surgery; and ways to prevent mice from infesting elaborate wigs.

ISBN 978 0 7123 5752 4 • 176 pages